WAKE UP

REDISCOVERING A PASSION
→ ● ←
FOR GOD AND THE BIBLE

STUDENT EDITION

A 31-DAY DEVOTIONAL EXPERIENCE

ANDY BLANKS

Published by: YM360

Wake Up: Rediscovering Your Passion for God and the Bible [Student Edition]

©2019 by Andy Blanks. All rights reserved.

Published by youthministry360.

ISBN:
10: 1935832859
13: 9781935832850

Any reference within this piece to Internet addresses of web sites not under the administration of the author is not to be taken as an endorsement of these web sites by the author; neither does the author vouch for their content.

Author: Andy Blanks
Art Director: Laurel Dawn Latshaw
Copy Editor: Paige Townley

"THE HOLY SCRIPTURE OF
ITSELF IS CERTAIN AND
TRUE;
GOD GRANT ME GRACE TO
CATCH HOLD OF ITS JUST
USE."
- MARTIN LUTHER

"RESTORE TO ME THE JOY OF
YOUR SALVATION . . ."
DAVID, PSALM 51:12

TABLE OF CONTENTS

INTRODUCTION

*"O GOD, YOU ARE MY GOD; EARNESTLY I SEEK YOU; MY
SOUL THIRSTS FOR YOU; MY FLESH FAINTS FOR YOU, AS
IN A DRY AND WEARY LAND WHERE THERE IS NO WATER."*

- PSALM 63:1

Have you ever in your life thought about God the way that David describes it in those verses up there? When you read this verse, do those words seem like words that would ever come out of your mouth?

If you can, if you can say that David's words here describe your day-in, day-out feelings toward knowing God, you probably don't need this book. Now, don't get me wrong: this book would probably still be helpful to you, for sure. But if you find yourself with a longing and thirst for God that leads you to seek Him each day through His Word, the angle this book takes may not hit you as squarely as it will others.

Because here's the deal: I can't read that verse and say that it has always described my feelings or actions when it comes to seeking to know God more.

I know, I know. I'm not really supposed to say that. After all, I'm pretty much a professional minister. I've been to seminary. I'm an author and a speaker. I have taught the Bible to teenagers and adults alike pretty much weekly for most of the past two decades. If anyone should have the whole "thirsting for God" thing down, it should be someone like me.

How is it possible that I haven't always seen myself in the words of this verse?

The longer I walk with the Lord, the more I can relate to this verse. More often than not, I feel like God's Spirit is right under my skin. God feels close, and I have a desire to draw even closer to Him.

But there have also been seasons when I would have read the verse above and it would have made me feel pretty rough. It would have reminded me of how far away I can feel from God. Maybe there have been times for you where you just couldn't seem to find the energy to read your Bible. Or you wanted to, but didn't know where to start. Maybe your prayers felt hollow. If this describes you, let me tell you that you're not alone. But I'm also here to tell you that there's a better way. Keep reading.

THE DISTANCE BETWEEN GOD AND YOU

There are a whole lot of reasons we feel distant from God. It's partly because of the way we live our lives. The lives many of us choose to live have very little space for God. We are booked solid. Our pace is intense! And when we DO have downtime that could be spent snatching moments of time with God, we're face down in a smartphone playing a game, watching Netflix, or catching up on Instagram or Snapchat.

Much of why we feel distant from God is spiritual. The Bible makes it clear that all of us are born with a sin nature (Rom. 3:23). We naturally tend to seek "self" and not God. Often we don't seek God because we won't seek God. The words of my favorite hymn, "Come Thou Fount of Every Blessing," come to mind:

"Prone to wander, Lord, I feel it, / Prone to leave the God I love."

For whatever reason, many of us will go through times in our lives when God simply feels far away. We don't sense His presence. He doesn't feel near. We see the way other people talk about their faith, and it seems as if they are describing an entirely different kind of journey than the one we're on. If this describes an experience you're familiar with, let me speak some encouragement to you for a moment.

Here is some real truth, so don't miss it: God is always near. He is never not near. God's nearness to you has nothing to do with you but everything to do with Him and His character. He is present in the lives of His children, and that's a fact. God is not distant. If you have been born again through saving faith in Jesus Christ, God is literally with you, within you, every moment of your life (Rom. 8:8-11). God can't be any nearer to you.

And yet, there are times in our lives when God truly feels far away. What do we make of this? The unfortunate truth is that when God feels far away from us, the root of the problem is not with God, but with us. If God feels distant, we have to look inside ourselves for what is causing the distance. This may not feel like me encouraging you. I get it. And yet, be encouraged! God is not far from you. He is never far from you! If this is true, it means that it is possible to feel close to Him. Again. Or maybe for the first time.

There is a wonderful promise in the New Testament, one I have depended on many times in my life. It's part of why I wanted to write this book for you. To help remind you of it. James 4:8 says, "Draw near to God, and he will draw near to you." Maybe you need to read that again. Read it 100 times if you need to. Do whatever you need to do for this powerful truth to take hold of your heart and mind. God is near. He is never not near. If you draw near to Him, He will reward your steps of faith, and He will remind you of His nearness.

If you feel far from God and take action to feel closer to Him, God promises us that you will feel God's nearness once again. I mean, I guess there could be more comforting promises in Scripture, but there have been times in my life when this promise has sustained me like few others. Maybe this truth is exactly what you need to hear today, too. I hope so.

But, there's still an issue. We know that God will honor our efforts to draw closer to Him, but what does drawing closer to Him look like?

How do we do it?

THE WAY BACK TO GOD

If you are like many people, you want to know God more and better, to feel a closeness with God, a passion for Him. But many teenagers often don't feel like their tried-and-true methods of seeking God produce these feelings. It's OK to admit it. I believe many young people find themselves here.

As Christ-followers, much of our lack of passion for seeking God is practical. For many of us, it boils down to this: we don't know HOW to seek God.

Read that last sentence again. It's important. What I am saying is that maybe you don't have a lack of desire, but a lack of know-how. Are you tracking with me? We like to think that we know all we need to know to seek after God, especially those of us who have grown up in church or who have been Christians for a while.

Many teenagers have a basic sort of understanding of what it means to read their Bible and pray. But I have come to believe that there are a ton of Christian teenagers out there, maybe teenagers just like you, who have never been really taught more than one or two ways to interact with the Bible. And it shows.

Study after study shows us a disappointing truth: American Christians live their lives separated from God's Word. The majority of Christians in the US don't read their Bible very much. Research all paints a similar picture. One study looked at the habits of all American adults and found that over 50% report reading their Bibles only three or four times a year. Only 14% of adults report reading their Bibles daily. Another study surveyed Christian adults, asking how many times they read their Bibles outside of church. Only 20% said that they read it daily, while another 20% reported that they never read their Bible outside of church.

What about teenagers you might ask? About the same. A study found that about 12% of teenagers read the Bible daily. That's not bad. But the largest category of teenagers was the 31% who reported reading the Bible about once a week. 19% reported reading the Bible a few times a year, if at all.

As a people, we are trying to live as Christians, but we are disconnected from the God-given source of what it means to live as a Christian.

I find myself asking why this is the case. I believe most Christians, especially most Christian teenagers, WANT to live in connection with God through His Word. But at the same time, I believe most Christians don't have a grasp of how to read the Bible, other than just reading a few verses here and there and trying to figure out how to apply them to their lives. Most Christ-followers have simply never been taught, and so it's easy for us to neglect the main way that God chooses to relate to us: the Bible.

We especially don't understand how to read the Bible in a way that feeds our hearts instead of our heads. What do I mean by this? Let me explain. Most people have only ever been taught to interact with the Bible in a way we might call "Bible Study." This is where you read a specific passage of Scripture, and you begin to analyze it. The goal is what we might call "understanding." We want to know what a particular passage says. And so, we read it. Depending on the resources we have at hand or our level of expertise, we may try to figure out the context of the passage, in other words, what's going on around it. If we're good at Bible Study, we take the knowledge we accumulate (the "what") and we seek to ask how it applies to our lives (the "why"). This is good Bible Study. But it can be pretty academic.

Now let me be clear: there's nothing wrong with this. Bible study on this level is useful, beneficial, and necessary. We need to know what God says. We need to be able, in the words of Paul, to "rightly divide" Scripture. We need to understand how to apply the teachings of the Bible to our lives. Studying the Bible in this way is a good thing. It's just not the only thing.

If we're honest, engaging with the Bible in the manner I just described doesn't always meet the desire we have to FEEL close to God. When God feels distant, when we're spiritually or emotionally tired, when we need to rediscover our passion, excitement, or joy for God, it's important to know that there are ways of interacting with the Bible that feed our emotional and spiritual needs. But so many people don't know how to do this.

I want to change this.

I believe that the key to rediscovering your joy for God comes through rediscovering, or discovering for the first time, your joy for meeting Him in the pages of the Bible. You see, the Bible is the primary way we meet with God. It's where we see Him giving us all that He believes we need to know about Him and His ways.

In this book, I want to teach you how to interact with your Bible in ways that will lead you to pursue God more and more. I want to help you see that reading the Bible doesn't have to be dull, dry, or academic. And more than anything, through approaching the Bible in ways that maybe you never have before, I want to help you rediscover your passion for God. That's my purpose in writing this book. I want to equip you to partner with the Holy Spirit to awaken your deep joy for God and His Word.

Throughout both the Old and New Testaments, when God is about to do something in the lives of His people, there is a cry to come awake.

> "Awake, awake, put on your strength, O Zion; put on your beautiful garments, O Jerusalem, the holy city; for there shall no more come into you the uncircumcised and the unclean." - Isaiah 52:1

> "Arise, shine, for your light has come, and the glory of the LORD has risen upon you." - Isaiah 60:1

> "But for you who fear my name, the sun of righteousness shall rise

with healing in its wings. You shall go out leaping like calves from the stall." - Malachi 4:2

"Besides this you know the time, that the hour has come for you to wake from sleep. For salvation is nearer to us now than when we first believed." - Romans 13:11

"For anything that becomes visible is light. Therefore it says, 'Awake, O sleeper, and arise from the dead, and Christ will shine on you.'"
- Ephesians 5:14

My prayer for you as you start this journey is that your soul would awaken. God is near you. He is always near you. I promise. Could it be that what you need is a better way to look for Him?

Maybe you are in a dark season when more than anything you crave God's presence in your life.

Maybe you find yourself simply longing for a fresh approach to encountering God in His Word.

Regardless, my prayer is that the practices in this book will WAKE YOU UP to a renewed love and joy for God and for who He is in your life.

HOW TO USE THIS BOOK

First, this book is designed to be read over a month. Some of you will work through this book in exactly 31 days. You are most likely the people who also organize their sock drawer by color. I am not making fun of you. OK, maybe just a little. But I think you are terrific, and I am thankful for you.

Most of you will need more than 31 days to go through this book. This is OK. Take your time. Go at your own pace. The important thing is to stick with it even when you don't feel like it. That's one of the wins in a book like this. If you've been struggling to meet with God regularly and are making a commitment to do so, God will honor you. He is faithful. He will meet you where you are. Along the way, you will find a new joy for meeting God in the pages of the Bible that you may never have experienced before.

Many of you will find that this book provides you with well over a month of content. Some of the experiences in this book are repeatable approaches to engaging with the Bible that can be applied to almost any passage of Scripture. If one of these approaches proves especially meaningful, you may choose to apply it to other passages of Scripture not suggested by this book.

Additionally, many of the Bible Study experiences contained in this book offer several options to choose from within that specific day's content. If you find that you really connect with a particular activity and that activity has a few different options, you may want to come back to that day's devotion and work through the options at your leisure.

Next, I would strongly encourage you to have a journal handy. Let me say that again: You need something to write with. I know that every phone has a notetaking app on it. And I know that Evernote and similar apps are wonderful tools for jotting down your thoughts. I love technology. But I am a firm believer that the act of writing is a crucial component of spiritual growth. The practice of writing down your thoughts forces you to slow down a bit and process information differently. You will be prompted in many ways throughout this book to write things down. I would encourage you to get a journal or a notebook in which to do it.

Finally, while I put a lot of thought into the order of the days in this book, and while I do believe that the optimal way of utilizing this book is to start on Day 1 and read in order through Day 31, you definitely don't have to do this. You can look at the table of contents and pick specific days that look the most intriguing to you and do them in the order you choose. That's an option available to you. If you decide to do this, let me ask you two favors:

- First, you'll notice Days 7, 14, 21, and 28 are slightly different days. These days are more action-oriented and are designed almost as a Sabbath of sorts from the other devotions. If you are going to read the book out of the suggested order (which is, again, fine to do), I would strongly encourage you to make it a point to do these days on the suggested timeline. (In other words, on your seventh day of reading, read Day 7, no matter what order you have read Days 1 through 6. Do the same with Days 14, 21, and 28.)

- Second, if you bounce around, commit yourself to read each of the 31 days. You're reading this book because you have a desire to re-connect with God through His Word. The main idea of this book is that there are exciting ways of connecting with God through the Bible that you may very well be unaware of. If you only pick days with titles that appeal to you, you will most likely miss out on a new way of meeting God in His Word that could very well be just the thing to inspire a more personal interaction with Him.

There will no doubt be days in this book that hit you better than others. I have tried every single one of the methods I propose in these pages. Some moved me greatly. Others not so much. But each of them is valuable in its own right. You never know how God will choose to speak to you. Be brave. Be open-minded. Give every day in this book the chance to make its mark in your life.

As you prepare to jump into Day 1, I want you to know that I am mindful of you. I do not know you. But this book was written prayerfully with you in mind. There is nothing special about this book. It is merely a resource that points to THE Book.

My prayer is that over the next 31 days or so, you will experience God and His Word in new ways and that through this, you will awaken inside of you a renewed joy for God. Now, let's get started.

THE NAMES OF GOD

PART 1

Do you know what your name means? I'd bet most people do. (In case you were wondering, my name, Andrew, means "strong and manly." I'm just tossing that out there.) The better question is whether your parents named you what they did because of its meaning or because of another reason. Maybe you share a name with a family member, or maybe your parents just liked the sound of your name. Whatever the reason, your name has come to mean something very specific. When someone who knows you hears your name, they immediately associate your name with the person you have come to be. Your name tells people who you are. Your name has meaning that has been established by the life you have lived.

It is no different with God's name. Interacting with God through the names He is given in the Bible is a powerful way to draw closer to God and to rediscover our passion for Him.

Today we're going to start with one of my favorite ways of interacting with Scripture to engage with God. This activity has helped me personally, and I've used it over the years to help others find meaning in it as well. We're going to focus our time of Bible reading by interacting with some of the different names of God.

Did you know that God has different names? It's true. One of the beautiful things about the Hebrew culture we see in the Old Testament is its remarkable use of names for God. The Hebrew authors used different names for God to describe the many different roles He played in their lives. For instance, in Judges 6:23-24, God came to Gideon in peace. And so, Gideon built an altar to God and named it "The LORD Is Peace," or in Hebrew, "Jehovah Shalom." The cool thing is that God's nature is unchanging, and so He still plays these roles in our lives today.

As we try to rediscover our passion for seeking out God through engaging with the Bible, really thinking about the names of God is a powerful practice.

In a moment, you'll encounter several names for God used by His people in the Old Testament. This grouping of names builds off the Hebrew word YAHWEH, the name God gave Moses when God met Moses in the burning bush. These names combine God's name with some of His attributes. The English translation of YAHWEH is "Jehovah." And so you'll see God's name, Jehovah, paired with one of His attributes.

HERE'S YOUR CHALLENGE FOR TODAY:

FIRST, set aside a time to pray over this list. We pray so that we can get our mind and spirit in a reflective, peaceful state, free from distractions.

THEN, read through the list a couple of times.

NEXT, choose one of the names of God from the list below that makes an impact on you. This could be a role God has fulfilled in your life in the past, or it could be a role He is playing now. Then, read the Bible verses where that name is mentioned and reflect on that aspect of who God is.

Here's a list of a few of the names of God:

Jehovah-Jireh: "The LORD will provide." This was the name used in conjunction with God providing a ram for Abraham to sacrifice in place of Isaac. This name is a testimony to God's deliverance.
> · Read Psalm 73:21-26.
> · Think about this: How has God provided for you in times of trial? How is He providing for you now?

Jehovah-Nissi: "The LORD is my banner." Moses ascribed this name to God after a victory over the Amalekites. The name of God was considered a banner under which Israel could rally for victory. The Lord's name was the battle cry.
> · Read Proverbs 2:1-8.
> · Think about this: How has God provided you victory in some area of your life? Where do you need that victory today?

Jehovah-Shalom: "The LORD is peace." This was the name of the altar that Gideon built at Ophrah signifying that God brings well-being, not death, to His people.
- Read Psalm 4:1-8.
- Think about this When has God been your peace in the past? Do you need His peace today in some way?

Jehovah-Rohi: "The LORD is my shepherd." God is the One who provides loving care for His people.
- Read Psalm 23:1-6.
- Think about this: What provision has God given you that you are most especially thankful for?

Jehovah-Rapha: "Jehovah Who Heals." Jehovah is the Great Physician who heals the physical and emotional needs of His people.
- Read Psalm 103:1-5.
- Think about this: How has God healed you in the past? What do you need healing from today?

Yahweh-Mekaddesh: "The LORD sanctifies." Holiness is the central revelation of God's character. God calls for a people who are set apart from the world to be used for His purposes.
- Read Psalm 40:1-3.
- Think about this: Give thanks to God that you've been set apart by God, cleansed of your sin, and made to be His child.

Yahweh-Sabaoth: "The LORD of Hosts." This can also be translated "the LORD Almighty." It represents God's power over the nations. The title sees God as King and Ruler of Israel, its armies, its temple, and of the entire universe.
- Read Psalm 66:1-7.
- Think about this: How do you see God's power displayed in the world around you? In your life?

FINALLY, pray to God using that specific name. (It's OK if you don't pronounce it correctly! God knows what you mean.) Thank God for realizing this role for you. Or, ask Him to help you see Him in this role.

The most important thing is keeping this concept in front of you throughout the day. As you can, reflect on this name. Consider writing it on your hand or a notecard. Do whatever you can think of to remember to focus on this name and how God relates to you in this way.

WHAT IS DEVOTIONAL READING?

I could barely hear my phone ringing. My beloved Auburn Tigers had just finished knocking off the second #1 ranked football team in as many weeks. What made this victory more special was that this was the Iron Bowl. We had just beaten our biggest rival, Alabama, in a game that was never really in doubt. The clock was winding down. Soon the fans would rush the field. My wife and I were screaming and cheering along with nearly 90,000 other Auburn fans. I felt my phone vibrating, and I saw that my mom was calling me.

I answered the phone knowing that I couldn't hear a word she was saying, and as I suspected, I couldn't. But I knew she would be screaming as loud as I was, and so I yelled back and let her hear the roar of the Jordan-Hare crowd for a moment. I hung up the phone and laughed. I could barely hear my wife next to me, much less my mom on the phone. There was too much noise.

Sometimes the distance we feel between God and us is caused by the noisiness of our lives. We have so much going on that even when we try to connect with God, we can't always hear Him over the "noise" we surround ourselves with. The goal of this devotion is to help teach us how to pursue God by quieting the noise in our lives.

Today's time of encountering God in the Bible embraces one of my favorite ways of engaging with Scripture. It's an ancient practice that comes from a time when most people in the Church were illiterate and relied on hearing the Word. I have found that as much as any one way of interacting with the Bible, this method speaks to my heart. Furthermore, I seem to be able to latch on to truths learned using this method. The echo of God's words stays with me longer if I can make the time to practice this approach.

The Latin phrase for this way of reading the Bible is "Lectio Divina." (Try to work the phrase into a random conversation today to impress your friends.)

That's a fancy way of saying, "devotional reading." Devotional reading is an experiential, heart-driven way of meeting God in the Word.

When we read the Bible in this way, we're not trying to do anything really scholarly. We're not taking a critical look at a passage. The sole point of devotional reading is to come to a relational, intimate interaction with God through the words you read. It asks the question, "What does God want to show me in these verses?"

If you've never read the Bible in this manner, if you think it sounds too emotional or mushy for you, I'd ask that you give it one chance. If you pour yourself into it, I promise you will be moved by what you get out of it.

HERE'S YOUR CHALLENGE FOR TODAY:

FIRST, find somewhere quiet. Quiet your mind. Prepare your heart. Slow down. Get yourself ready to meet God in His Word. Start with a prayer to God, asking Him to show you what He has for you in this passage.

THEN, read the passage. You can use the one I have included below or choose your own. Read it slowly, almost word by word. The idea is to read as if God is going to stop you and show you something at any moment. As you come across words or phrases that seem to speak to you, pause and focus on them. Think about what it is about them that speaks to you. But most of all, listen to what the Spirit is trying to show you.

NEXT, think about the passage even deeper by reading it one more time, but this time, read it out loud. (This might feel strange at first, but it's an essential part of processing the passage in a way that allows you to pick up on different cues rather than merely reading it to yourself.) This time, really soak in the words and ideas you're encountering. If God wants you to think on certain things, do so. Allow the words to guide your interaction with God.

THEN, you need to think about your response. This is your chance to engage in a conversation with God. Pray to Him, asking Him what He wants to show you. Express to Him how the truths He led you to reflect on made you feel.

FINALLY, summarize to yourself what you have learned. Some people like to jot these thoughts down in a journal. Some can do this mentally. But the idea is to spend some time – however much you spend is up to you – just thinking about what God has shown you and how it changes who you are. Try to hone in on specific concepts that you can take away.

I want to challenge you to give this method an honest try, even if it feels new or a little unusual. The passage I've chosen for you to read today is Romans 8:31-39. Go ahead and jump into this time of devotional reading.

"[31] What shall we say about such wonderful things as these? If God is for us, who can ever be against us? [32] Since he did not spare even his own Son but gave him up for us all, won't he also give us everything else? [33] Who dares accuse us whom God has chosen for his own? No one—for God himself has given us right standing with himself. [34] Who then will condemn us? No one—for Christ Jesus died for us and was raised to life for us, and he is sitting in the place of honor at God's right hand, pleading for us.
[35] Can anything ever separate us from Christ's love? Does it mean he no longer loves us if we have trouble or calamity, or are persecuted, or hungry, or destitute, or in danger, or threatened with death? [36] (As the Scriptures say, "For your sake we are killed every day; we are being slaughtered like sheep.") [37] No, despite all these things, over whelming victory is ours through Christ, who loved us.

[38] And I am convinced that nothing can ever separate us from God's love. Neither death nor life, neither angels nor demons, neither our fears for today nor our worries about tomorrow—not even the powers of hell can separate us from God's love. [39] No power in the sky above or in the earth below—indeed, nothing in all creation will ever be able to separate us from the love of God that is revealed in Christ Jesus our Lord. – Romans 8:31-39 (NLT)

A DIFFERENT TAKE
ON PRAYER

Prayer is the language of our relationship with God, but for many of us, our prayer lives are often lacking passion or feeling. Does this describe you sometimes? We pray to God, and maybe we thank Him for the blessings He has given us. Perhaps we remember to pray for other people. But if we're honest, many of us are too quick to pray for our own needs and the things that concern us most. None of this is wrong in itself. But too often, we don't pray to God with the kind of worship and passion that He desires us to bring to Him.

Have you ever felt like your prayers bounce off the ceiling? Like they don't even make it to God? If you do, you're not alone. I believe many people find prayer to be something they struggle to know how to fully engage in. And yet, meaningful prayer to God is often linked to reading the Bible. When we can see God clearly in the Bible, we should be moved to speak to Him in ways that communicate the awe and wonder of who He is. This exercise will help you begin to do just that.

This day's exercise will blend the two main ways God has given us to come to know Him: prayer and Scripture reading. Today you're going to use the Psalms as a way of reaching out to God in prayer.

Praying through the Psalms is a powerful way to seek God using the words of Scripture. There are so many powerful thoughts and emotions in the Psalms. When we pray to God using the words of the Psalms as our own, it helps us connect with God in a way that maybe we haven't before. So today you're going to pray through a specific psalm, personalizing it as a way of speaking to God in the language of His Word.

This approach can be applied with any passage of Scripture, but I'll provide one for you for this time of prayer. After engaging in the practice, try it out on another passage or two.

HERE'S YOUR CHALLENGE FOR TODAY:

FIRST, start by praying to God to help you clear your mind and heart.

THEN, begin reading the psalm below as it appears in your Bible.

NEXT, pray through the psalm as if it were your own words, slowly and authentically expressing the thoughts as your own. Think about what you're saying to God. Take your time. (If you want, pray it all over again!)

What does this look like? Let's use Psalm 100 as an example. Start by reading Psalm 100 slowly. Then, pray through it, personalizing it as you go. This is an example of what I mean by personalizing it. It might go something like this:

> *"God, I shout for joy to you. I join all the earth in praising you.*
> *I worship you with gladness; I come before you with joyful songs.*
> *I know that you, LORD, are God. It is you who made me, and I am*
> *yours; I am the sheep of your pasture.*
>
> *God, I enter your gates with thanksgiving and your courts with praise;*
> *I give thanks to you and praise your name.*
>
> *For you, LORD, are good and your love endures forever; your faithfulness*
> *continues through all generations."*

THEN, listen. As much as time will allow, just sit and reflect in silence, focusing on being in God's presence.

FINALLY, close your prayer as you see fit.

Try this with Psalm 100 or try it with another one of the psalms. (You may find that Psalm 29 and Psalm 46 are particularly meaningful for this exercise.) When you're finished, grab a journal and record your thoughts.

Did this prayer experience feel different?

Did you feel like your prayers were more meaningful?

What was positive about it?

What about it did you not feel comfortable with?

The Lord longs to communicate with us. Prayer is how we do this. As you go throughout your day, be sure to make time to meet with God in prayer.

THINKING ABOUT WHO GOD IS

PART 1

As you start another day's devotion, I pray that you are finding that your hunger to know God through His Word is growing. I pray that you have found some new ways of meeting God in the Bible. And I pray that you are beginning to be excited about your time spent in the Bible. If these things are true for you, this is a sure sign that you're growing in your passion for God.

Today's activity is fun. Today you're going to do two things: spend some time thinking about one of God's attributes and use Scripture as a guide for praising God.

If I asked someone close to you to describe you to me, how long would it take them to move past your physical description and begin to describe your characteristics? Would your friends say you were funny? Would your mom or dad talk about how kind you are to others? Would a coach or teacher tell about how hard you work to improve? Our attributes define who we are. Or maybe who we are defines our attributes. (Tough to say exactly how the order works.) Regardless, the point is this: because they know us, the people in our lives know how to act around with us. They know how to connect with us. The same can be true for how we approach God.

When we encounter God, we do so with a sense of who He is in mind. We come to Him with expectations because of who He is. We may not always realize it, but what we know about God flavors every aspect of our interactions with Him. We are confident because we understand who God is. We know His attributes, and therefore, how to engage with Him.

What do we mean when we say "God's attributes"? God's attributes are simply His characteristics. Pretty simple. But there are two pretty cool truths about God's characteristics: He is perfect in all of His attributes, and His attributes are unchanging.

First, God is perfect in who He is. So when we say that God is loving, we mean that He is perfectly loving. When we say that God is good, we mean that He is perfectly good. As we seek to rediscover our joy for knowing God, it's important to know that He is worthy of our affection. Worthy in every way.

Second, God is unchanging. He is eternal. The way He is, He has always been. In his book The Attributes of God, Arthur Pink wrote, "Everything about God is great, vast, incomparable. He never forgets, never fails, never falters, never forfeits His word." I love this repetition at the end of that quote. It speaks to the fact that God is unchanging.

Reflecting on God's character and knowing that it is perfect and unchanging is such a powerful way to rediscover our passion for God. The great 19th-century Baptist preacher Charles Spurgeon once wrote:

"The word, the character, and the actions of God should be evermore before our eyes; we should learn, consider, and reverence them. Men forget what they do not wish to remember, but the excellent attributes of the Most High are objects of the believer's affectionate and delighted admiration."

Reflecting on God's nature through encountering Him in His Word leads us to affection and admiration.

HERE'S YOUR CHALLENGE FOR TODAY:

FIRST, look below. There you will see some of God's attributes accompanied by verse references. Then, choose an aspect of God's character that jumps off the page at you. Here's a partial list of God's attributes (we'll do this again with the rest of God's attributes on Day 17):

God's Goodness
  · Psalm 16:2, 31:19, 86:5, 119:68, 143:10, 145:7, 145:9

God's Truthfulness
  · Psalm 25:5, 26:3, 40:10-11, 43:3; John 14:6

God's Faithfulness
  · Exodus 34:5-7; Deuteronomy 7:9, 32:4; Psalm 36:5, 89:5, 115:1, 117:2

God's Holiness
· 1 Samuel 2:2; Psalm 22:3, 30:4, 99:3, 99:5, 145:21; Revelation 15:4

God's Forgiveness
· Psalm 25:11, 32:1, 79:9, 86:5, 130:4; Matthew 6:12; Ephesians 1:7; Daniel 9:9

God's Righteousness
· Job 37:23; Psalm 7:17, 11:7, 35:28, 36:6, 103:17, 111:3

NEXT, search some of the verse references. You can certainly read them all if you want, but identify two or three that are especially meaningful to you.

THEN, use these verses as a guide to praising God. How? Speak these verses back to God using His Word to bring praise to Him. (It's similar to how we prayed through the psalms earlier in the week, but this is praise.) The actual biblical phrase for this is "ascribing praise to God." Ascribing praise is telling God something about Himself that He already knows and owns.

Here's an example of how this might look: if I chose God's Goodness as the attribute I wanted to focus on, and I looked up Psalm 31:19, it would say, "Oh, how abundant is your goodness, which you have stored up for those who fear you and worked for those who take refuge in you, in the sight of the children of mankind!" My prayer might sound something like this: "Father, I praise you because you are good. I praise you that your goodness never runs out. Your goodness is abundant! Thank you for storing it up for me. You are my refuge. I praise you that you are good in your love and care for me." Or something like that.

FINALLY, be mindful of this aspect of God's character as you go through your day. This is important: let these verses be on your heart and mind. Praise God throughout the day for this specific attribute. Remember Him for who He is.

STORING UP GOD'S
WORD IN YOUR HEART

Words from people we know and respect can be life-giving, can't they? I can still remember my high school football coach encouraging me before a big game. I can remember my dad teaching me the importance of hard work when I was growing up. He'd say, "Most things worth having are worth working hard for." I remember words spoken to me by mentors, by friends, by my mother, and many encouraging words spoken by my wife. Words have power. They keep us going. They guide us.

This is never truer than when it comes to God's Word. The Bible itself says that God's Word is like a lamp guiding our path (Ps. 119:105). The Bible is given to us so that we can know God. And the goal isn't just collecting knowledge. It's that we would know God and know how to live our lives in a godly way.

Knowing this is true, the question then becomes: How well do we know God's Word? For many of us, this is a convicting question.

With this as our backdrop, today's devotional experience focuses on the act of "storing up God's Word in your heart." I didn't say memorizing Scripture because, if you're like me, there can be some baggage here. I have always struggled with memorizing Scripture. It's not something that comes easy to me, as much as I hate to admit it. But I have always wanted to be good at it.

The problem for me is that there have been times in my life when I have felt like memorizing Scripture was kind of an emotionless experience. I have had seasons where I couldn't get the energy up for it. Now, this says more about me than it does about the practice of memorizing Scripture.

I think my issue was one of motivation. When memorizing Scripture is hard for me, is it because my motivation is more about doing something I know I need to do as a good Christian? Or is my motivation more about wanting to experience God more? The attitude that we bring to this practice will depend a ton on our motivation.

In Psalm 119:11, David said, "I have stored up your word in my heart, that I might not sin against you." Stored up your word in my heart . . . That's a cool description of a relationship with God's Word. The purpose David offered for doing this was personal holiness ("that I might not sin against you"). But there are other purposes for knowing God's Word. For our purpose, we want to know God's Word so that we can rediscover our passion for God. To that point, I have chosen some verses that I think would be awesome for you to try and memorize. (But feel free to find a passage of your own.)

Remember, our goal is to grow in our passion for God. Storing up God's Word in our hearts and using it as a way to think on certain truths throughout our day is a powerful way to do this.

You may have your own tested and tried method of doing this. And there are some great apps out there that help, too. But this is a method that really has worked for me. Maybe it will work for you as well. It's simple, and I would encourage you to give it a try today. Here's how it works. (You'll need your journal again, or a scratch piece of paper.)

HERE'S YOUR CHALLENGE FOR TODAY:

FIRST, prayerfully reflect on the verse. Read through the list below slowly, thinking about the power behind each of these verses. Here's your list of verses:

Exodus 15:2
"The LORD is my strength and my song, and he has become my salvation; this is my God, and I will praise him, my father's God, and I will exalt him."

Psalms 73:26
"My flesh and my heart may fail, but God is the strength of my heart and my portion forever."

Proverbs 3:5-6
"Trust in the LORD with all your heart, and do not lean on your own understanding. In all your ways acknowledge him, and he will make straight your paths."

Proverbs 18:10
"The name of the LORD is a strong tower; the righteous man runs into it and is safe."

Isaiah 41:10
"Fear not, for I am with you; be not dismayed, for I am your God; I will strengthen you, I will help you, I will uphold you with my righteous right hand."

John 14:27
"Peace I leave with you; my peace I give to you. Not as the world gives do I give to you. Let not your hearts be troubled, neither let them be afraid."

John 16:33
"I have said these things to you, that in me you may have peace. In the world you will have tribulation. But take heart; I have overcome the world."

Romans 15:13
"May the God of hope fill you with all joy and peace in believing, so that by the power of the Holy Spirit you may abound in hope."

Philippians 4:6-7
"Do not be anxious about anything, but in everything by prayer and supplication with thanksgiving let your requests be made known to God. And the peace of God, which surpasses all understanding, will guard your hearts and your minds in Christ Jesus."

Psalm 147:11
"But the LORD takes pleasure in those who fear him, in those who hope in his steadfast love."

THEN, find a verse that speaks to you. Choose that verse as the one you will store up in your heart.

NEXT, read the verse five times very slowly, working on remembering the phrasing and cadence of the words, but also, trying to internalize the truth behind the verse's meaning.

THEN, write the verse on a piece of paper until you can do it five times without looking.

FINALLY, say the verse aloud until you can do it five times without looking. If you can do this, you've got it.

One final word: Follow-through is huge when it comes to storing up God's

Word in our hearts. One thing that has been helpful to me over the years is to write the verse on a notecard and stick it in my pocket. And on the bathroom mirror. And on my car's dashboard. And on the fridge. And make it the phone's screen saver . . . See what I'm getting at? Visual reinforcement is an important aspect of knowing God's Word.

Also, remember that our goal is not to collect knowledge but to engage with God through His Word. If we never look at or think about this verse again, we've blown it! Do what you have to do to focus on this verse throughout the day.

FOCUSING ON THE PROMISES OF GOD

PART 1

Throughout the Bible, God clearly and powerfully says who He is and what He will do for us. These are His promises. This is the first of two devotional experiences in which you will spend time interacting with God through the promises He has made to us, His children.

Our goal is to be people who approach God's Word the right way; it's important that we don't try to make the Bible say something it doesn't. Focusing on God's promises can sometimes lead Christ-followers to put words in God's mouth, or to try and make certain verses fit a situation they were never intended to fit. We must have a really good framework ahead of time before we jump into our look at the promises God has made.

There are essentially two types of promises in the Bible: promises God makes to specific people at a specific time, and "general" promises God makes to all people. Many of the specific promises were made to Israel during a unique period of God's salvation history. But there are a ton of promises God makes that, based on context, apply to ALL of His people for all time. I've pulled some of these more general promises out for our two devotional times. Moving forward, you may enjoy searching for more of God's promises in Scripture on your own.

Before we jump in, I want to share four principles of God's promises with you. I know, I know . . . this feels like a lot. But it's SUPER important. There are a lot of Christ-followers who walk around upset at God because they don't understand how God works. Especially when it comes to His promises. I don't want that to be you. After all, I want this activity to draw you nearer to God. If there is any misunderstanding about how God works through His Word, it could have the opposite effect. So, consider these four principles before you jump into today's devotional experience.

1. God is faithful. God is perfectly faithful. (For a list of verses referencing God's faithfulness, refer to our first devotion on God's attributes on Day 4).

God will always do what He says He will do. Always. In some of Joshua's final words to the Israelites, he reminded them of the faithfulness of God:
"And now I am about to go the way of all the earth, and you know in your hearts and souls, all of you, that not one word has failed of all the good things that the LORD your God promised concerning you. All have come to pass for you; not one of them has failed." - Joshua 23:14

The Israelites could count on God's faithfulness to keep His promises. So can we.

2. God's ways are higher than our ways. God will always keep His Word, but God often fulfills His promises to us in ways we may never be able to understand. This is because God's ways aren't our ways. Isaiah 55:8-9 says, "For my thoughts are not your thoughts, neither are your ways my ways, declares the LORD. For as the heavens are higher than the earth, so are my ways higher than your ways and my thoughts than your thoughts." Sometimes God allows us to understand how and why He keeps His promises to us. Sometimes He doesn't. This doesn't change who God is.

3. God is sovereign. Sovereign is a big word that simply means God is in charge of everything. No one overrules Him. Let me ask you a question: have you ever used your parents' promise against them to make them do something that they may not really want to do? "Mom, you promised we could go to the mall and shop for shoes!" Of course, this is followed by your mom's stunning realization that she did, in fact, make that promise (What was she thinking?!) and a grudging acknowledgment that she will keep her promise to go shopping. God doesn't operate this way.

We can't twist God's arm into keeping a promise in the same way you can sometimes twist your parent's arm. God is sovereign. He is the Creator King over all things. While He is faithful in keeping His promises, He will do so according to His will, which is "good, acceptable and perfect" (Rom. 12:2).

4. God always has eternity in view. We hold on so tightly to the life we live on this earth. It's hard for us to realize how fragile it is. This world is not our home. The life we live here, though it may seem like it is the pinnacle of our existence, is shockingly brief compared to the eternal life God promises we will live with Him. God fulfills His promises with eternity in mind. Sometimes, God keeps His promises not in our temporary life on earth, but in our forever-life with Him.

HERE'S YOUR CHALLENGE FOR TODAY:

FIRST, read the list of promises below and the accompanying Scripture.

THEN, find the one promise that speaks to where you are in your life right now. What promise leaps off the page at you? What situation do you find yourself in where you need God to show up in a specific way? Identify the promise below that is most relevant to your life today. Here's your list of some of God's promises:

God promises to provide a way out of temptation.
"No temptation has overtaken you that is not common to man. God is faithful, and he will not let you be tempted beyond your ability, but with the temptation he will also provide the way of escape, that you may be able to endure it." - 1 Corinthians 10:13

God promises to be our strength.
"He gives power to the faint, and to him who has no might he increases strength. Even youths shall faint and be weary, and young men shall fall exhausted; but they who wait for the LORD shall renew their strength; they shall mount up with wings like eagles; they shall run and not be weary; they shall walk and not faint." - Isaiah 40:29-31

God promises He will be with you in tough times.
"When you pass through the waters, I will be with you; and through the rivers, they shall not overwhelm you; when you walk through fire you shall not be burned, and the flame shall not consume you." - Isaiah 43:2

God promises to give us wisdom.
"If any of you lacks wisdom, let him ask God, who gives generously to all without reproach, and it will be given him." - James 1:5

God promises He is near to us if we draw near to Him.
"Draw near to God, and he will draw near to you . . . " - James 4:8

God promises salvation through faith.
"For God so loved the world, that he gave his only Son, that whoever believes in him should not perish but have eternal life." - John 3:16

God promises that His presence will drive out fear and uncertainty.
"It is the LORD who goes before you. He will be with you; he will not leave you or forsake you. Do not fear or be dismayed." - Deuteronomy 31:8

God promises to meet our needs.
"And my God will supply every need of yours according to his riches in glory in Christ Jesus." - Philippians 4:19

God promises that He works for our good.
"And we know that for those who love God all things work together for good, for those who are called according to his purpose." - Romans 8:28

NEXT, prayerfully think about how specifically the promise you've chosen impacts your situation. How does it make you feel? What does the promise offer you? How does this promise change the way you think about where you find yourself? What might be some of the possible ways, considering your situation, in which God keeps His promise?

THEN, spend some focused time in prayer, bringing both God's promise and your specific situation before God. Thank God for His faithfulness and His sovereignty. Tell God that you trust Him to keep His promise even though you may not get to see or understand how exactly He does it. Confess to God your belief in His perfect will and tell Him that you know He will fulfill His promise to you in a way that is in line with His character.

FINALLY, memorize the verse (or verses) that contain the promise you've chosen. Keep it in front of you today and in the future. Look for how God will answer your promise. Expect Him to! And be ready to acknowledge Him in praise and thankfulness when He does.

WHAT IT MEANS TO FAST

"Fasting is a divine corrective to the pride of the human heart. It is a discipline of body with a tendency to humble the soul." - Arthur Wallis

Fasting. When you hear the word, do you think of a practice that is only for the super-religious? Does it seem like something ancient? Something out-of-step with our twenty-first-century lifestyle? I bet that many people reading this either wrinkled their noses when they saw this heading or skipped it altogether. I believe that many people feel like fasting is too extreme to be a part of their regular faith habits. I hope that if you have any sort of hang-up about fasting, or that if you've never tried it before, you'll come to see it as an amazing tool for cultivating a surprising closeness with God.

Let's spend just a couple of minutes or so talking about what fasting is and what fasting isn't. In its simplest form, fasting is simply not eating for a defined time period. (Though there are other kinds of fasting, as we'll see later in this book.) If you look at fasting in the Old Testament, Israel's leaders would often make everyone fast in response to God's judgment or disfavor and they "were always accompanied by prayer and supplication and frequently by wearing sackcloth as a sign of penance and mourning." This isn't the kind of fasting we're necessarily talking about here.

The interesting thing is that we don't see Jesus commanding His followers to fast. But, the way Jesus spoke about fasting to His disciples implies that it was something they were already doing. However, there still seems to be an aspect of mourning or repentance in the kind of fasting His followers would have been used to doing. And so Jesus, as He did with many aspects of faith, reframes fasting into a practice that is less about legalistically following Old Testament tradition and more about drawing closer to God.

Jesus shows that He desires our fasting to be less about religious ritual and more about connecting with God. In Matthew 6:16-18, Jesus said, "And when you fast, do not look gloomy like the hypocrites, for they disfigure their faces that their fasting may be seen by others. Truly, I say to you, they have received their reward. But when you fast, anoint your head and wash your face, that your fasting may not be seen by others but by your Father who is in secret. And your Father who sees in secret will reward you." Jesus was doing here what He did best. He was transforming religious practice from a detached and potentially legalistic approach to God to a personal and intimate one.

The truth is that Jesus didn't really tell us a specific way of fasting. He modeled it in the 40 days He spent in the wilderness before being tested by Satan, but even this example, taken in context, isn't Jesus necessarily prescribing a specific roadmap for us to follow. We have to read between the lines at how the New Testament addresses fasting to get a sense of how it was being practiced.

So what does the Bible say about fasting? In Luke, we see a description of fasting tied to worshiping God. Anna, the aged prophetess who recognized the baby Jesus as Messiah in Luke 2:36-38, was described as never departing from the temple, "worshiping with fasting and prayer night and day." We know that John the Baptist's followers fasted. And in Acts 13, the church at Antioch showed that fasting played a role in this church body's worship and decision-making. Paul and Barnabas further demonstrated that fasting also played a role in important decisions in Acts 14:21-23. But that is almost all that we have in the biblical record of fasting.

What we know from Church history is that fasting was something really common in the early Church in the centuries following the events recorded in the Bible. It is an important practice that has been passed down for thousands of years and one that we would do well to make a part of our spiritual lives, especially if we find ourselves feeling distant from God.

In Celebration of Discipline, Richard Foster wrote, "Fasting must forever center on God. More than any other discipline, fasting reveals the things that control us." Fasting from food is one way of prayerfully and worshipfully centering our attention on God. Let's talk about how this will look for you today.

HERE'S YOUR CHALLENGE FOR TODAY:

FIRST, decide when you will fast and for how long. Most people who fast do so by not eating food for one day (still drinking water or even juice). Prayerfully decide what works for you, then make sure your parents or another adult is aware of what you're planning. There's no reason to be reckless in how you do this. If you're going to run a marathon, it's probably not the best day to pick to fast. Be wise. While fasting is designed to "inconvenience" us, we want the experience, especially if it is a new practice, to be meaningful. Don't set yourself up for failure if it's a practice you're unfamiliar with (like fasting on the day of your big family reunion).

NEXT, start your day off with an extended time of prayer and reflection. I have found this to be an important part of the process. It sets the spiritual tone for your day and puts you in the position to hear what God wants to tell you.

FINALLY, fast! Here is the key to fasting: whenever you are hungry throughout your day, focus your attention on God. Let your body's need for food remind you of your need for God. If possible, during your normal lunch break, have a time of prayer or Scripture reading. And most of all, be joyful that you are spending so much time focused on God.

LEARNING FROM THE CHARACTERS
OF THE BIBLE

PART 1

Think of a skill you've developed throughout your life. While there are some skills you can pick up without someone else helping you, many of the things we know how to do were taught to us at some point by someone else. I can still vividly remember my dad teaching me how to drive a car on country roads outside of the town in which I grew up. I remember my brother teaching me to play guitar. I learned how to build a house from a guy named Ken Ward. I could go on and on.

What about you? Did your mom teach you how to cook? Did your dad teach you how to tie a tie? Did your granddad teach you how to fish?

So many skills in our lives were taught to us by other people. Often this comes in the form of modeling. We watch someone do something a few times, and then we try it ourselves. Ideally, they are there to correct us here and there. Before long, we're doing it on our own.

Part of why God gave us Scripture is to show us how people just like us interacted with Him so that we would model our lives and our faith after their example. Think about it: God could have just given us a list of all His commands. "Do these specific things. Don't do these things." But He didn't. He gave us a story instead. Part of this is so that we can learn from the example of others.

You'll be surprised how interacting with people from Scripture can awaken your passion for God and His Word. Learning about the lives of people who had these crazy interactions with God helps us live our lives. We can be encouraged because most of these people made mistakes just like we do. We see ourselves in them. Their example can also strengthen us. Seeing how they dealt with both loss and gain while staying true to God empowers us to follow their example.

Most importantly, we see in these biblical characters the story of how God interacts with His people. For those of us who find ourselves feeling discon-nected from God or who are struggling with our excitement about reading the Bible, engaging with God through the lens of the characters of the Bible may be just the thing we need to reawaken our souls to the wonder of how God engages with His people.

HERE'S YOUR CHALLENGE FOR TODAY:

FIRST, prayerfully read the list of people below. Maybe you see a favorite character you want to revisit. Maybe you see a name or two whose story you aren't as familiar with. Whichever direction you want to take, choose a char-acter from the following list:

Abraham - Father of the Israelites. Husband to Sarah. Father to Isaac.
- Main Passage: Genesis 11-25
- Other Places: Exodus 2:24; Matthew 1:1-2; Acts 7:2-8; Romans 4; Ga-latians 3; Hebrews 2, 6-7, 11

Caleb - One of 12 men sent by Moses to secretly survey the land of Canaan. Only Caleb and Joshua had faith that God could deliver the Israelites.
- Main Passage: Numbers 13-14:38
- Other Places: Numbers 32:11-12; Joshua 14:6-15

Elijah - One of the most famous of Israel's prophets. Defeated prophets of Baal. Landed on the bad side of King Ahab and Queen Jezebel.
- Main Passages: 1 Kings 17:1-2; 2 Kings 2:11
- Other Places: Matthew 11:14, 16:14, 17:3-13, 27:47-49; Luke 1:17, 4:25-26; Romans 11:2-4; James 5:17-18

Isaiah - One of the greatest of Israel's prophets.
- Main Passage: Isaiah 6
- Other Places: 2 Kings 19:2-20:19, Matthew 3:3, 8:17, 12:17-21; John 12:38-41; Romans 10:16-21

John the Baptist - Jesus' cousin. Prophet called by God to prepare the way for Jesus.
- Main Passages: All four Gospels
- Other Places: Isaiah 40:3; Malachi 4:5; Acts 1:5, 22, 11:16, 13:25, 18:25, 19:3-4

John the Apostle - Called the "beloved disciple." Wrote Gospel of John, 1, 2, and 3 John, and Revelation.
- Main Passages: All four Gospels, Acts, and Revelation.

Joshua - Powerful leader of Israel. Took over for Moses. Led Israelites into the Promised Land.
- Main Passage: Book of Joshua
- Other Places: Exodus 17:9-14, 24:13, 33:11; Numbers 27:18-23, 32:11-12; Deuteronomy 3:28, 14, 31:7; Judges 2:6-9

Moses - Author of the first five books of the Bible. God's chosen deliverer of the Israelites from Egyptian slavery. Sin kept him from entering the Promised Land, but he was a faithful leader of God's people.
- Main Passages: Exodus through Deuteronomy
- Other Places: Acts 7:20-44; Hebrews 11:23-29

Noah - Chosen along with his family to live through the Flood. God called him righteous. Not perfect, but faithful.
- Main Passage: Genesis 5:28-10:32
- Other Places: Isaiah 54:9; Hebrews 11:7; 1 Peter 3:20

Peter - Unofficial leader of the disciples. Impetuous but passionate. Denied Christ but was forgiven by the resurrected Jesus. Delivered sermon at Pentecost. Prominent New Testament leader.
- Main Passages: All four Gospels and Book of Acts
- Other Places: Galatians 1:18, 2:7-14; 1 and 2 Peter

Rebekah - Wife of Isaac. Mother to Jacob and Esau. Beautiful. Welcoming. Her actions surrounding Jacob receiving Isaac's blessing are troubling.
- Main Passages: Genesis 24, 25:19-28
- Other places: Genesis 27

Ruth - Faithful daughter-in-law to Naomi. Wife to Boaz. Great-grandmother to David.
- Main Passage: Book of Ruth
- Other Places: Matthew 1:5

Stephen - Helped distribute food in the Jerusalem church. First Christian martyr.
- Main Passage: Acts 6:3-8:2
- Other Places: Acts 11:19, 22:20

THEN, with a journal or a note-taking app handy, begin to read about them. Some of the characters have stories that span chapter after chapter of the Bible. Some are mentioned only in a few verses. Wherever you find yourself, read the story of the character you have chosen.

NEXT, when you have finished, ask yourself the following questions:

- What did I learn about God in this story? How do I see God interacting with this person? Where do I see God's perfect plan shine through in this person's life?

- What did I learn about the specific person? What positive traits did they show? What kind of person do they seem to be? What, if any, weaknesses revealed themselves? How did they approach God?

- What can I learn about myself? Where do I see lessons to be applied to my own faith life? How would I react if put in the place of the character? What about this person's story exposes something in me that needs to change or be strengthened?

When you've finished, spend some time in prayer, listening to what God has to say to you and thanking Him, once again, that He chooses to reveal Himself to His people rather than staying aloof or unknown. Praise God for His great love and mercy that compel Him to engage so thoroughly with us, His creation.

FINALLY, marinate on this character's story for the next few days. Go back to it in your mind. Keep mining it for the truth about God and yourself.

THINKING ABOUT
GOD'S BLESSINGS

As humans, we're good at life when it's going well. We're at our best when life is easy. I'm a joy to be around when I'm caught up at work, the bank account is (relatively) full, my kids are healthy, my wife is happy, and I've gotten my workout in for the day. I'm a likable guy on those days. Catch me when my wife and I have had a spat, or the pile of bills is greater than the number on my mobile banking app, or heaven forbid there's a tragedy. Then maybe I'm not quite as agreeable. We're all a little guilty of this. It's human nature. But it doesn't mean it's right.

Here's a truth that you and I both would do well to pay closer attention to: our lives are rich with the blessings of God, even if we don't always recognize it. James 1:17 says, "Every good gift and every perfect gift is from above." Every good thing. Not some. Not most. Every. If there is even a sliver of good in your life, even the smallest bit, it is a gift from God. A blessing.

Are you aware of your blessings? Do you consistently look around you at the good in your life and credit it to God? This, as much as anything in this book, is central to rediscovering a passionate love for God. Growing this attitude of awareness and gratitude toward God and His blessings will awaken in you a deeper love for the Lord. I want to help you do that today.

(It wouldn't be cool of me if I didn't speak to those of you reading this who are in the midst of a dark time. I do not want to paint over the fact that you may very well be reading this and be hurting really badly. Maybe you have just lost a loved one or received some tragic news. You may be grieving over something you have lost. Grief is a part of what it means to be human. It is not an emotion foreign to God. God is the originator of our emotions, and Scripture is full of examples of God meeting the messy grief of His children. And even grieving Himself. If you're hurting right now, I'd like your permission to gently suggest that even in your pain, that a position of awareness and gratitude for God's blessings is for you, too. In fact, let me say from experience that in the midst of great sadness, focusing on even the smallest good gift from God may be the thing that pulls you through.)

In today's devotional experience, you're going to be meeting God and acknowledging Him as the source of your blessings (through engaging with Scripture), while also expressing your thankfulness for the blessings He's given you.

HERE'S YOUR CHALLENGE FOR TODAY:

FIRST, get in a mindset where you can talk to and listen to God. Pray that the Spirit would help you get in a place to have a meaningful time with the Lord.

THEN, look up one or more of the following verses. Read the passages more than once, reflecting on God as the giver of good things. Here are your verses:
- Psalm 34:10
- Psalm 91:14-16
- Psalm 103:2-5
- Psalm 111:5
- Psalm 145:15
- Matthew 6:26, 30-33
- Luke 12:22-31
- 1 Corinthians 2:9
- 2 Corinthians 9:8-10
- Philippians 4:19

NEXT, take a moment and either jot down the blessings God has given you or mentally note them. Take your time on this, reflecting on God's blessings, thinking about your health, your family, your best friend, your hobbies, where you live, your favorite song, the warmth of the sun, or even your favorite color (seriously). Reflect on the joy these blessings give you.

THEN, go to God with a thankful heart, telling Him the joy that His blessings bring you. Praise Him for the favor He has shown you. Take your time.

FINALLY, take the verse(s) you chose and do whatever you have to do to reflect on it again throughout the day. Keep it on your phone, write it on a scrap sheet of paper, put it in your car, or put it on your bathroom mirror. Do what you need to do to focus on this aspect of God today.

I pray that this reflection on God and His blessings changes your outlook for today.

FOCUSING ON THE THEMES
OF THE BIBLE

The Bible is many things. It is history. It is poetry. It is prophecy. It is wise moral teach-ings. It is the truth about the nature and character of God. It is a practical guide for Christian living. It is all these things and more. The Bible is such a powerful resource because of the many different ways in which it speaks to us. I pray that part of what this book is doing for you is helping you see new ways of interacting with the Bible. And I pray that this is breathing new life into your relationship with God.

One of the many ways of approaching God in a new and more meaningful way through His Word is by tracing any one of the various themes through the Bible. You may call this practice a "theme study." A theme study is simply where you take a theme, any theme, and read about it as it comes up throughout Scripture.

Now, as you may be thinking, these can get pretty in-depth. You could spend months reading about God's love. Or grace. Or God's compassion. You get the point. But today's devotional will help you do a relatively short theme study. How-ever, my encouragement to you is to make time in the future to engage with God in this way more frequently. It can make a HUGE impact on your understanding of who God is and how He works.

How do you do a theme study? How do you know what themes are in the Bible? You can do a theme study by using an online Bible search engine like biblegate-way.com, esv.org, or by searching on your Bible app. You can also go old school and use the concordance in the back of your printed Bible. Regardless, the first step is to search for a keyword or a concept.

While countless themes course through Scripture, some of the main themes in the Bible are grace, love, holiness, any of God's attributes that we've listed in this book, judgment, redemption, salvation, reconciliation, adoption, faith, the trinity, sin, and so on. A search on the Internet for "Bible themes" is a great place to start.

Once you've done your word search, I like to look for passages that answer three general questions:

1. Where do we see this word or concept in God's character?
2. How do we see this concept fulfilled or completed through the lens of Jesus and the Gospel?
3. What are some verses that speak to us about living this concept out in our lives?

For today, I've chosen a theme search for you to get started with: a look at the theme of "holiness."

HERE'S YOUR CHALLENGE FOR TODAY:

FIRST, and as always, pray and ask God to help settle your thoughts and give you a spirit of discovery. Pray that the Spirit will open your eyes to what He wants to reveal to you.

THEN, read through some or all of the verses below. Spend some time prayerfully answering the three questions I mentioned above: where you see this concept in God, where you see Jesus bring this concept forward, and how we are to live it out. Here is your list of verses:

- "The LORD is in his holy temple; the LORD's throne is in heaven; his eyes see, his eyelids test the children of man." - Psalm 11:4

- "Yet you are holy, enthroned on the praises of Israel." - Psalm 22:3

- "Ascribe to the LORD the glory due his name; worship the LORD in the splendor of holiness." - Psalm 29:2

- "Sing praises to the LORD, O you his saints, and give thanks to his holy name." - Psalm 30:4

- "For our heart is glad in him, because we trust in his holy name." - Psalm 33:21

- "Your way, O God, is holy. What god is great like our God?" - Psalm 77:13

- "I appeal to you therefore, brothers, by the mercies of God, to present your bodies as a living sacrifice, holy and acceptable to God, which is your spiritual worship." - Romans 12:1

- "Even as he chose us in him before the foundation of the world, that we should be holy and blameless before him." - Ephesians 1:4

- "Put on then, as God's chosen ones, holy and beloved, compassionate hearts, kindness, humility, meekness, and patience." - Colossians 3:12

- "But as he who called you is holy, you also be holy in all your conduct, since it is written, 'You shall be holy, for I am holy.'" - 1 Peter 1:15-16

FINALLY, take comfort in the fact that there is no real description for exactly what this looks like. You may reflect on this theme and these questions for 15 minutes or so, and that will be enough for you. You may spend two or three days thinking about this list of verses. Take your time and let God lead you.

Being able to trace how God works throughout the Bible is a powerful way of reconnecting with God through His Word. Make sure you close your time in Bible reading today by praying to God and thanking Him that He makes Himself and His ways knowable to us, His children.

SEEING GOD'S WORD

On my desk, there is a picture of my wife. It is a tightly cropped black and white photo. You can barely make out the silhouette of her face through her wedding veil. The light plays off her lips and catches her right cheek and chin. If I look closely, the irises of her blue eyes look almost white in the picture. She is magnificently beautiful.

I keep this picture and others of my children on my desk for the same reason you keep pictures of people you love: I want to recall them. My wife and my children are my greatest earthly joys. I like having them present in my office. Because of my love for them and the value I place on the roles they play in my life, I have them integrated into my daily world.

I want us to consider today what it means to take a step toward a similar integration of God in our lives.

Now unless you know something I don't know, you don't have a picture of God to put on your desk. But we have been given something just as personal as a picture. We have been given God's Word. As we strive to see our relationship with God come alive, having God's Word near us is a powerful tool.

Part of why God seems distant to some of us is because we keep Him at a distance. Unlike other meaningful relationships in our lives, we don't create for ourselves reminders of God to connect with throughout our day. I want to challenge you to change this.

As I have stated previously, God's Word is the primary way He has made Himself known to us. As we increase our passion and engagement with His Word, we increase our knowledge of Him. And with the Spirit working to grow a hunger for God within us, the more we encounter God, the more we want to encounter Him.

Today's challenge is to come up with creative and practical ways to make God's Word more visible in your daily life.

HERE'S YOUR CHALLENGE FOR TODAY:

FIRST, take the time to read Deuteronomy 6:4-8. Deuteronomy 6:4-8 is commonly referred to as the Shema (pronounced "shuh-MAH"). The Shema was for centuries the Jewish statement of faith, of which Deuteronomy 6:4-8 is one part. (Many orthodox Jews still recite the Shema daily.) It's a powerful passage rich in truth and application.

Notice how the passage talks about God's Word. It is to be in our hearts. It's to have a place of importance in our family discussions and identity. And we're to incorporate it into our daily lives in a very visual and real way. The Jews in biblical times went as far as to take this command literally, making little boxes containing tiny scrolls of Scripture they would tie to their foreheads and wrists! While I don't want any of us walking around with boxes on our heads, I would like to challenge you to bring God's Word out of the Bible and into your surroundings in a similar way.

How does this look? That's up to you. But here's some guidance:

- Start by identifying verses that are meaningful to you or have been meaningful in your life.

- Then, think of ways you can give these verses visibility in your daily life.

- This can be as simple as writing the verses on the back of note cards and taping them to your bathroom mirror, but you can also get creative with it.

- There are a million apps you already use for creating images. Use what you already use, except use it to make God's Word come alive. Save your images as your screensaver on your phone, or your desktop on your computer.

- Acrylic 4x6 picture frames are great ways to display Scripture. Trace the frame on plain paper, cut out a few templates, and

write verses on them. Put the frame in your kitchen, on your bathroom counter, etc.

· Search Pinterest for "bible verses." You'll find a ton of visual repre-
sentations of Bible passages. Find some you like and save them on
your phone to use as your screen saver. Or, download them and
print them out.

· Search for Instagram accounts that feature creative Scripture. There
are a lot of them. Make it a habit to check these accounts regularly
and meditate on what you read.

The ideas are endless and are only limited by your creativity. But the point is
intentionality. If you don't make it a priority to make God's Word more visually
prevalent in your life, you won't do it.

Don't miss the opportunity to make God more present in your daily life by
making His Word more present.

WAKE UP

DAY

TWELVE

REMEMBERING GOD'S
FAITHFULNESS

As humans, we have a perspective problem. And it's super difficult for us to do anything about it. The problem with our perspective is complicated. First, we tend to look at the world around us through the lens of "self." In other words, we process the daily events of our lives based on how they impact us. Second, we tend to only think in terms of recent history. Because our world is so fast-paced, we don't stop a lot and think about the big-picture story of our lives. This is especially true when it comes to our past. We're pretty much laser-focused on the here and now and how it impacts us today.

The only problem with this is that we miss out on various and often dramatic ways that God has intervened in our life.

Our goal is to be people who have a joy for God. For this to be true about us, we must learn how to slow down and reflect on how God has intervened in our lives. The Bible, and especially the psalms, gives us some pretty cool instructions for what this looks like. The faith of God's people in the Old Testament was expressed so often when they got together and remembered what God had done for them.

Think of someone in your life that you love. Someone who makes you smile just thinking about them. I bet a part of your affection toward them is based on shared experiences: fun stuff you've done with them, tough times you've walked through alongside them, unique experiences you've shared, and so on. It's no different with God. I am certain that you could point to specific times in your life when God showed up in a way only He could. Do you make it a point to remember these moments and thank God for them? You should. We all should. And today you will have a chance to do just that.

Psalms is full of examples of people recalling a time when God interposed Himself in their lives, and they praised Him accordingly. We're going to use one of these psalms to guide us in voicing thankfulness and praise to God through recalling times when God interjected Himself into your life.

HERE'S YOUR CHALLENGE FOR TODAY:

FIRST, as always, is to prepare your heart and mind to engage with God. Whether you're sitting in a coffee shop or reading this before you go to bed, this is as simple as saying a prayer and clearing your mind.

THEN, read one of the psalms below, focusing on how the author voiced praise to God for a time when God did something awesome in their life or the lives of God's people. Read the psalm again, maybe even several more times. Pay attention to the emotional expression of thankfulness. Here are a few passages to consider:

Psalm 100

"[1] Make a joyful noise to the LORD, all the earth! [2] Serve the LORD with gladness! Come into his presence with singing! [3] Know that the LORD, he is God! It is he who made us, and we are his; we are his people, and the sheep of his pasture. [4] Enter his gates with thanksgiving, and his courts with praise! Give thanks to him; bless his name! [5] For the LORD is good; his steadfast love endures forever, and his faithfulness to all generations."

Psalm 111

"[1] Praise the LORD! I will give thanks to the LORD with my whole heart, in the company of the upright, in the congregation. [2] Great are the works of the LORD, studied by all who delight in them. [3] Full of splendor and majesty is his work, and his righteousness endures forever. [4] He has caused his wondrous works to be remembered; the LORD is gracious and merciful. [5] He provides food for those who fear him; he remembers his covenant forever. [6] He has shown his people the power of his works, in giving them the inheritance of the nations. [7] The works of his hands are faithful and just; all his precepts are trustworthy; [8] they are established forever and ever, to be performed with faithfulness and uprightness. [9] He sent redemption to his people; he has commanded his covenant forever. Holy and awesome is his name! [10] The fear of the LORD is the beginning of wisdom; all those who practice it have a good understanding. His praise endures forever!"

Psalm 77:10–15

"[10] Then I said, 'I will appeal to this, to the years of the right hand of the Most High.' [11] I will remember the deeds of the LORD; yes, I will remember your wonders of old. [12] I will ponder all your work, and meditate on your mighty deeds. [13] Your way, O God, is holy. What god is great like our God? [14] You are the God who works wonders; you have made known your might among the peoples. [15] You with your arm redeemed your people, the children of Jacob and Joseph."

Other passages you may consider: Psalm 103:1-5, Psalm 132, and Psalm 136.

NEXT, stop for a moment and think about a time or times when God moved in your life. Think of a time when you knew, beyond a shadow of a doubt, that God had intervened to work for His glory and your good. Maybe it was an answered prayer. Maybe it was looking at a beautiful sunset and recognizing it as the work of God. Maybe God comforted you in a time of despair. Whatever the case, really focus on this intervention. Think about exactly how you felt God's presence in your life. If you have a journal handy, describe the event(s) in as much detail as you care to.

FINALLY, voice or write a prayer of praise and thankfulness to God, telling Him how awesome He is and how thankful you are for His intervention.

I have two final thoughts with which I want to challenge you. First, if you do this once today and then move on, you'll find that you miss opportunities to continuously dwell on God's faithfulness. Find a way to remind yourself to think about this throughout the day. Second, try writing your prayer of thanks to God on a scratch sheet of paper, notecard, or even a note app. Place it somewhere prominently to look at to remind you of God's faithfulness.

WAKE UP

DAY
→ ● ←
THIRTEEN

UNLOCKING YOUR
CREATIVE SIDE

I have a theory. The reason we don't always seek God may not be because we have a flaw in our character; it may be because we have a flaw in our behavior. We are simply so committed to our busy schedules that we don't make time to properly meet God in His Word. I chose the word properly for a reason. Sometimes we will grab a few moments of God in the margins of our lives, in the car on the way to school, or reading a couple of verses while we get ready in the morning. While this kind of drive-by engagement with Scripture is a great way for staying in touch with God, it's no substitute for a dedicated time alone focusing on God's Word with no distractions.

Today's method is designed to MAKE you slow down and think about the God with whom you so eagerly want to reconnect. It's a lot different than how some of you are in the habit of interacting with Scripture. But if done properly, it has some real advantages.

Today's devotional time is a way of engaging with God's Word called the "creative" method. Like some of these other ways of meeting God in the Bible, this may be your first time doing something like this. This particular method seemed a little juvenile the first time I had someone lead me in it. But, it turned out to be a way of engaging with God that has worked for me over the years.

I'm a visual learner, and maybe you are, too. For me, these simple icons help anchor my mind on what God is trying to show me. So even if this feels a little outside of your comfort zone, I'd like to challenge you to give it a shot.

Remember, the idea is that you want to grow in your hunger for knowing God. Experimenting with different ways of meeting God through Scripture is a great way to do this. So give the creative method a shot and see how it hits you.

HERE'S YOUR CHALLENGE FOR TODAY:

FIRST, prayerfully read the passage below. I have included this passage for you to apply this method to, but you can use any passage of your choosing. Here's the suggested passage:

> "[1] So if there is any encouragement in Christ, any comfort from love, any participation in the Spirit, any affection and sympathy, [2] complete my joy by being of the same mind, having the same love, being in full accord and of one mind. [3] Do nothing from selfish ambition or conceit, but in humility count others more significant than yourselves. [4] Let each of you look not only to his own interests, but also to the interests of others. [5] Have this mind among yourselves, which is yours in Christ Jesus, [6] who, though he was in the form of God, did not count equality with God a thing to be grasped, [7] but emptied himself, by taking the form of a servant, being born in the likeness of men. [8] And being found in human form, he humbled himself by becoming obedient to the point of death, even death on a cross. [9] Therefore God has highly exalted him and bestowed on him the name that is above every name, [10] so that at the name of Jesus every knee should bow, in heaven and on earth and under the earth, [11] and every tongue confess that Jesus Christ is Lord, to the glory of God the Father." - Philippians 2:1–11

THEN, when you've finished reading the passage once, re-read the passage, asking yourself these questions and drawing the appropriate symbol in your Bible or journal:

- A lot of times, God puts the same idea in front of us over and over again when He is trying to teach us something. Is there a recurring truth that God has been showing you lately? If so, draw a circle beside the phrase.

- Did God reveal anything to you in this passage that was convicting or that spoke to your heart? Draw a heart beside the word or phrase that God used to impact the way you feel about an aspect of your faith.

- Is there something you don't understand? A confusing concept? Draw a question mark beside this, and then commit to asking your parents, a youth leader, or a mentor about the concept.

· Is there a powerful or meaningful concept that God brought to your mind? Draw an exclamation point beside that word or phrase in your Bible.

· Many times, Scripture compels us to take action. Is there something in this passage that God is using to encourage you to take action in your life? Draw an arrow by that phrase.

FINALLY, as you'll often be encouraged to do in this book, make sure you do something to keep these concepts in front of you today. Maybe it's as simple as drawing a heart or question mark (or whatever symbol you've associated with what God is trying to teach you today) on your hand. Or, if that's not for you, jot the same symbol down on a notecard or a scratch sheet of paper.

Simple, right? The idea is that the visual cue helps you in keeping the passage's meaning close to you throughout the day.

Before you wrap up, spend some time in prayer, praising God for who He is and thanking Him that He has revealed such relevant truth to you in His Word.

WHAT IT MEANS TO FAST
FROM MEDIA

At the end of our first week of devotions, you fasted from food to help you focus on God. Today I'm going to encourage you to embrace a different kind of fast. I'm going to challenge you to fast from media today. Huh? Let me explain.

What I am challenging you to do today is to take a 24-hour break from Instagram, Snapchat, Twitter, YouTube, Netflix, TV, browsing the Internet for entertainment purposes, and so on. If this causes you a little panic, or better yet, if you immediately think I'm a lunatic for even suggesting it, this may very well be just what the doctor ordered.

Have you ever watched a talented magician in person? Maybe it was someone doing card tricks or tricks with a coin. I love watching magicians who have perfected their craft. The sleight of hand it takes to pull off the illusions magicians practice is amazing. But magicians will tell you that the success of a good magic trick often relies on a very important concept: misdirection.

Wikipedia defines misdirection as "a form of deception in which the attention of an audience is focused on one thing in order to distract its attention from another." Misdirection takes many different shapes: hand flourishes, facial expressions, quick movements, and so on. But the goal is the same: the idea is to focus your attention on one thing while the actual trick happens unnoticed. Misdirection hinges on an important truth, namely, that most people can only focus their attention on one thing at a time.

In our entertainment rich culture, media serves as spiritual misdirection. If you are like me, most of the "free" moments of my day are spent engaged with media. When I am in the car, I listen to an audiobook or a podcast or Jason Isbell and The 400 Unit. When I'm waiting in line in the grocery store, I glance at Instagram. I may check Twitter while I'm waiting to pick my daughter up from volleyball practice. Or I watch a video news story on the USA TODAY app. Is any of this inherently bad? No, it's not. But without boundaries and intentionality, all of this can act as spiritual misdirection, leading me to focus all of my attention on entertainment leaving no time for reflection on God.

Ask yourself this: How often do you spend the moments of downtime in your day praying to God instead of turning to media? How often do you spend your "free" moments reflecting on a Bible verse or a spiritual concept?

Here's a better question: If you spent as much time in prayer or meditation as you did on social media, how would your relationship with God change?

Convicting questions, aren't they? They are for me even as I write this. And I bet they are for you as well.

Against this backdrop, I want to strongly urge you to spend a full day fasting from media. (If you're feeling super brave, try a full-blown technology fast, abstaining from all forms of technological entertainment for one day.) Like your fast last week, you will use your constant desire for media to prompt reflection on God.

HERE'S YOUR CHALLENGE FOR TODAY:

FIRST, choose when you want to fast from media. For those of us whom we might call "super users," this is going to impact your day and maybe your psyche. Some of you may need to prepare yourself for what you're about to do. If you're someone who spends a significant amount of time on social media, it may help to lessen your anxiety by announcing on your preferred social media channels that you're going to fast from media for a day.

THEN, in the words of Nike, "just do it." Spend a day fasting from social media. Anytime I fast, I like to make sure I start the day with a meaningful time of prayer and reflection in silence and solitude. It helps me prepare mentally and spiritually for the fast. I would encourage you to start your day in this manner, praying a specific prayer: ask God to use the moments throughout the day when you are tempted to engage with media as prompts to encourage you to engage with Him instead.

I would encourage you to choose a psalm of praise to guide your time spent on God during your fast. I'd recommend Psalm 113, included below, but feel free to choose one that speaks to you.

"[1] Praise the LORD! Praise, O servants of the LORD, praise the name of the LORD! [2] Blessed be the name of the LORD from this time forth and forevermore! [3] From the rising of the sun to its setting, the name of the LORD is to be praised! [4] The LORD is high above all nations, and his glory above the heavens! [5] Who is like the LORD our God, who is seated on high, [6] who looks far down on the heavens and the earth? [7] He raises the poor from the dust and lifts the needy from the ash heap, [8] to make them sit with princes, with the princes of his people. [9] He gives the barren woman a home, making her the joyous mother of children. Praise the LORD!"

REMEMBER, this won't be easy for some people. That's the point. The goal is that this practice highlights a) our increasing dependency on things that serve as "misdirection" and b) our need to focus on God more throughout our days.

If you successfully fast from media for a day and in its place spend meaningful time engaged with God in prayer and reflection, your desire and joy for God will be awakened. It will not be time wasted.

GETTING EMOTIONAL

Have you ever been really excited about an answered prayer? Maybe you made the team after a competitive tryout. Maybe you passed a test you didn't think you'd pass. Or maybe a loved one survived a cancer diagnosis. Whatever the case, you prayed, and God answered.

Have you ever felt joy at recognizing God's power as Creator when you looked at something beautiful in nature? I know I have, countless times. Seeing a beach sunset on Alabama's Gulf Coast, hiking in the backcountry of the Grand Tetons in Wyoming, watching a powerful storm blowing across the Kenyan plains . . . I experienced joy in God's creative works in each of these situations. Maybe you have had an encounter with God and experienced excitement, joy, happiness, gratefulness, or any other emotion. These encounters lead us to experience God in richer ways, waking us up to His glory and sovereignty.

However, there are other emotions we direct at God, emotions that are very different from the ones just described. Have you ever been angry with God? Have you ever been disappointed? Has God ever allowed something to happen that caused you great pain? Have you felt frustration at a prayer that wasn't answered in the manner you wanted it to be? Have you ever gone to God in confusion because of an outcome or turn of events? If the answer is "yes" to any of these questions, don't worry. It doesn't make you wrong. It makes you human.

We often feel positive emotions directed toward God because of who He is in our lives. The negative emotions we feel toward God don't change who God is. And while these negative feelings can make us not feel like we want to be close to God, they don't change the fact that God is always near to us. God is not offended by our emotions, no matter how raw. God is the Creator of emotions. He can handle anything we bring to Him, and the truth is that He wants us to send our emotions His way. He doesn't shy away from even our most intense feelings.

Today, as we continue our journey of awakening our hearts and minds to the richness of God, let's think about our emotional relationship with God. Before you flip the page to another day, let me assure you, I am not the poster boy for emotional reflection. I tend to lean toward the less emotional end of the spectrum, and yet, I realize that it's important to tap into the emotional side of our engagement with God. It's a vital aspect of our relationship with Him, both when things are going well and when they aren't.

Today you're going to have a time of intentionally focusing on your emotional reaction to God and His presence in your life. The Bible is full of examples of people bringing their emotions to God, maybe none more consistently than David, who expressed a range of emotions to the Lord. We'll look at a very select number of them today as a way of guiding us in this process. But I want to challenge you to consider how we see people in Scripture express their emotions. If you devote time to thinking about it, you'll realize there is a deep record of people bringing all manners of emotion to God, some of which may shock us in the depth of their expression.

HERE'S YOUR CHALLENGE FOR TODAY:

FIRST, spend some time in prayer, reflecting on your relationship with God over the last season of your life. How has God intersected with your life in ways that brought you joy or peace? Have some things caused you to feel pain or frustration or maybe even hopelessness toward God? Be honest with yourself and with God. God knows your thoughts anyway. Psalm 139:1-2 says, "O LORD, you have searched me and known me! You know when I sit down and when I rise up; you discern my thoughts from afar." You're not keeping anything from God by not expressing it. Spend some time thinking about your emotional reaction to God's presence in your life.

THEN, begin the practice of bringing these emotions before God. For the positive emotions, this is easy. We have an understanding of what this looks like. Praise and thankfulness are easy and come fairly natural. We may struggle knowing how to bring our anger, disappointment, and despair before God. The good news is that Scripture gives us a model.

Below you will see a list of places in Scripture where people expressed their emotions to and maybe even about God. Browse the list below. Find an emotion or emotions that are similar to the emotions you're dealing with. Read the passages and use the examples you see there for a model of how you will confess your emotions. (Even if you don't find the exact emotion that describes how you're feeling, the principle is the same.)

- Moses' frustration and confusion in Numbers 11:10-15
- Hannah's joy in 1 Samuel 2:1-2
- Naomi's grief in Ruth 1:11-14
- Elijah's disappointment and despair in 1 Kings 19:1-18
- David's fear in Psalm 55:4-8
- David's weariness and sorrow in Psalm 6
- David's thankfulness in Psalm 9:1-2
- David's desire for vindication in Psalm 26
- David's guilt in Psalm 51
- Asaph's frustration with God in Psalm 74
- David's praise to God for His presence in Psalm 106
- Mary's joy in Luke 1:46-56
- Jesus' sorrow and fear in Matthew 26:36-42
- Paul's hope and courage in Philippians 1:19-20

FINALLY, spend some time openly confessing your emotions to God. For some of you, this will be relatively brief and easy. Excitement and hopefulness are easy to bring before the Lord. It will be harder to bring the more intense emotions of hurt or loss to God. But give God a chance to be God. Be honest in your pain or frustration, knowing that God hears our cries and cares deeply about our pain.

Talk to God openly today. Be honest. Be raw. It's not sinful to express in faith your genuine hurt to God. He wants the burden. He never shies away from His children's pain.

The goal of this practice is to open yourself to a more authentic relationship with God, one that He has empowered not only through His great love for you, but through His intimate nearness to you and all His people.

Go to God today, knowing that your emotions are safe with Him.

LISTENING TO GOD'S WORD

Have you ever received a text or a DM on Instagram where you couldn't tell if someone was mad at you or not? You read the words or tried to decipher the emojis, trying to figure out if this person was simply in a hurry or whether or not you've done something to frustrate them.

Why no emoji?

Is that "lol" ironic, sarcastic, or are they really joking?

They usually include a gif. Why no gif?

They never use gifs. Why a gif this time?

In the twenty-first century, we've become experts at having to read between the lines of our digital communication.

Now compare this with the sensation we get from talking directly to someone. There are still plenty of quirks to our communication, but it's way easier to tell someone's mood by hearing their voice. The challenges we face in figuring out someone's mood mostly disappear in face-to-face conversation. We process hearing a person's voice differently than we do reading it.

The same thing is true when we listen to Scripture being read. When we listen to the Bible read aloud, we often process the words differently than when we only read them. We pick up on different parts of the text. Certain points stand out to us when we hear the passage out loud. Our brains may even process the text differently by hearing it; many people find they can remember a passage better because they have heard it being read rather than just reading it.

Remember that our purpose behind this book is to rediscover a real desire to know God and meet with Him in His Word. Listening to the Bible is a powerful way to supplement reading it. If you find that your Bible reading routine has grown somewhat stale, it's a really simple and yet powerful way to wake up your time in Scripture. The result is, of course, that you would know God more and better as a result.

The great thing about listening to the Bible is how easy it is with modern technology. Years ago, if you wanted to listen to a recording of someone reading the Bible aloud, you'd have to buy a version on CD, upload it to your computer, and then figure out how to get that content on your various devices. Today, the apps we have on our phones have awesome audio versions available. For free. That's tough to beat.

HERE'S YOUR CHALLENGE FOR TODAY:

FIRST, if you haven't already, download the YouVersion app by Life.Church. It's by far the most popular Bible app in the world—so popular that you almost certainly have it on your phone already. Whether or not you've noticed it yet, if you're looking at a specific passage, at the bottom of your screen there is a little speaker icon. Click that, and boom . . . you're listening to Scripture. (NOTE: YouVersion also has a browser-based application if you can't listen on your phone. I also use the ESV Bible app from Crossway. It has an audio feature as well.) I know other apps have this feature and countless websites that offer it, Biblegateway.com being the most prominent. However you access it, the goal today is to find a way to listen to Scripture.

NEXT, get somewhere you can listen and not be interrupted. I have to confess that sometimes I listen to Scripture in the car in the mornings between dropping my kids off at school and arriving at my office. It's one of the few times in the day when I truly have no interruptions. Whatever works for you, make sure you can concentrate on really listening to the passage you're focusing on.

THEN, decide what you will listen to. Maybe you listen to a passage your pastor preached on or that you studied in youth group. Maybe you have a Bible reading plan you're working on. Or, maybe you just browse through Psalms or Proverbs looking for something that speaks to you. However you go about it, pick a passage to focus on.

NEXT, listen to the passage. Listen to it once to get the hang of the rhythms and cadence of the speaker. Then, listen to it again and begin to focus on the truth of the passage. Finally, listen to it at least one more time. This time, note specific aspects of the passage that stand out to you. Write these down in a journal or note-taking app.

FINALLY, when you have listened to the passage enough times that you have captured what God wants to show you, spend some time reflecting on the truths you've just heard. If this is new to you, it may surprise you how easily you recall verses and phrases and how you're able to recall them throughout the day. (It's part of the beauty of hearing God's Word written and why listening to God's Word being read has been part of the Church experience since Old Testament times.)

Reflect on what these truths mean for your life. How do they change the way you see God? How do they impact your faith? Do they call you to action? Do they speak to your values? How do you feel after reflecting on God and His ways as you have? Be sure to spend time in prayer, processing this with God, being sure to listen to what He has to show you.

Consider making listening to the Bible a regular part of your relationship with God.

MEDITATING ON WHO GOD IS
PART 2

This is the first of a few devotional experiences in this book that have a "part 2." Why? Simple. There was just too much good stuff for one devotion. It's not surprising that God's attributes is the first one of these two-parters. Of all the ways in which you have approached God in this book and all the ways you will, thinking about who God is maybe the most satisfying.

Our goal for this book is for you to rediscover a passion for your relationship with God. There may be no better way to do this than by spending time really thinking about who God is.

Today is another chance to reflect on God's attributes. It's a different list than Day 4, but the process is the same. You're going to meditate on one of God's attributes and use Scripture as a guide to praising God.

Just to remind you, when we say "God's attributes," it's just another way of describing the various characteristics of who God is. Recall that we said that God is perfect in all of His attributes, and His attributes are unchanging. That's important as we seek to know and love God. We can completely rely on Him to be who He is, fully, and to ALWAYS be this way.

God's perfection and His unchanging nature are directly related to our ability and desire to know and love Him. Spend some meaningful time deeply thinking on God's attributes today so that you may love, worship, and obey Him more.

HERE'S YOUR CHALLENGE FOR TODAY:

FIRST, look below. There you will see some of God's attributes accompanied by verse references.

God's Power
Deuteronomy 3:24, 7:21; Psalm 62:11, 29:3; Nahum 1:3; Isaiah 26:4

God's Majesty
Psalm 8:1, 93:1, 104:1, 145:5; Job 37:22; Isaiah 2:10

God's Omniscience (All-knowing)
Psalm 147:5; Matthew 6:8; Isaiah 55:8-9; Romans 11:33; Job 37:16; Jeremiah 10:12

God's Justness
Job 12:22; Psalm 37:27-29; Ecclesiastes 3:17; Romans 1:18-32, 3:23, 5:8-11; Hebrews 10:30

God's Sovereignty
Psalm 103:19, 115:3, 135:5-6; Proverbs 16:33; Ephesians 1:11-12

God's Omnipresence (Everywhere, Infinite)
Genesis 1:1; 1 Kings 8:27; Psalm 139:7-18; Isaiah 66:1; Romans 11:33; Hebrews 13:8; Revelation 1:8

THEN, choose an aspect of God's character that strikes you as meaningful based on where you are in this season of your life.

NEXT, look up some or all of the verse references. Identify two or three that are especially meaningful to you.

THEN, use these verses as a guide to praising God. How? Speak these verses back to God using His Word to bring praise to Him. (It's similar to how you prayed through the psalms earlier in this book, but this is praise.) The actual biblical phrase for this is "ascribing praise to God." Ascribing praise is telling God something about Himself that He already knows and owns.

Here's an example of how this might look:

If I chose God's Power as the attribute I wanted to focus on, and I looked up Nahum 1:3, it would say, "The LORD is slow to anger and great in power, and the LORD will by no means clear the guilty. His way is in whirlwind and storm, and the clouds are the dust of his feet."

My prayer might sound something like this: "God, I praise you that you are slow to anger and great in power. Thank you for your powerful justness that sees the guilty punished and your mercy that showers us with forgiveness. You are powerful! Your way is in whirlwind and storm, and the clouds are the dust of your feet. I praise you and stand in awe of you, God."

FINALLY, be mindful of this aspect of God's character as you go through your day. This is important: let these verses be on your heart and mind. Praise God through-out the day for this specific attribute. Remember Him for who He is.

HAND WRITING SCRIPTURE

Every once in a while, I find myself dealing with a challenge. Someone will ask me to write a message on a birthday or thank you card or something similar, and I will come to the realization that writing is not something I am very good at! I create with words for a living, but I would guess that 97% of the words I create are typed on my laptop. I rarely write long passages by hand, and when I have to do it, I realize how out of practice I am. In those moments, it's like I'm asking my brain to wake up a part of itself that has been asleep. My dependence on technology means that typing is my preferred way of getting words on paper (er . . . screen).

Maybe you can relate, but there is an interesting truth about the act of writing: various studies show that the act of writing leads to better information retention and overall learning. One study showed that students who leaned on writing as the primary way of learning a foreign language picked up the language quicker and retained more words. One study on goal setting found that people who hand write their goals are more likely to achieve those goals than people who don't. One study even found that students who write notes in class are more likely to remember them than students who type them.

Writing out any information by hand seems to create a more lasting relationship with that information than merely typing it. The brain activity and motor skills it takes to write seem to lead to a more familiar understanding of the content. The interesting thing to me is that this seems to be supported by Scripture.

In Deuteronomy 17, an interesting passage crops up. After a discussion of the various feasts God wanted His people to keep in the Promised Land, there is a section that speaks to people in authority. Moses recorded God making an allowance for the people to name for themselves a king. After Moses outlined this, he wrote the following (emphasis mine):

> "And when he sits on the throne of his kingdom, **he shall write for himself** in a book a copy of this law, approved by the Levitical priests. And it shall

be with him, and he shall read in it all the days of his life, that he may learn to fear the LORD his God by keeping all the words of this law and these statutes, and doing them, that his heart may not be lifted up above his brothers, and that he may not turn aside from the commandment, either to the right hand or to the left, so that he may continue long in his kingdom, he and his children, in Israel." - Deuteronomy 17:18-20

Isn't that interesting? God wanted the kings that would rule over His people to know His law. This makes sense, and from a scholarly approach, the main idea here is that the kings appointed by God to rule would rule according to God's Word and ways. But I think it's pretty awesome that God specifically wanted the kings to copy the Law themselves.

What was God getting at? Why not have a scribe copy the Law? Why make a copy at all? Why not just use the existing version in whatever form it was in? I believe God is showing us something here. I believe there is significance in God commanding the kings to intentionally invest themselves in pouring over the Law, line by line, and writing a new copy of it. I believe God knew that such a personal interaction with His Word would help the kings better grasp the heart of God's commands.

Have you ever devoted any significant time to writing passages of Scripture? If you have, you will know what many others know: there is nothing quite like this practice for helping you know the ins and outs of God's Word. Hand writing verses of Scripture unlocks a fresh familiarity with the text.

I have had seasons in my life when I approach the Bible, and no matter how I try, I can't seem to get myself in a position to let the words I'm reading sink in. In these times, it's as if there is a barrier to a deeper connection with Scripture. I can read the Bible, and when I step away, it's almost as if I haven't read it at all. If you can relate to this, I want to offer you a huge encouragement: writing passages of Scripture is a powerful way to break through this type of disconnect with God's Word.

If you have never tried this practice, I want to strongly encourage you to do so today. It may very well be the simplest form of interacting with Scripture mentioned in this book. And I promise you from experience that the return is worth the investment. After all, if it was good enough for the kings of Israel, it should be good enough for us, right?

HERE'S YOUR CHALLENGE FOR TODAY:

FIRST, pray. Pray that God would settle your spirit and clear your mind. Pray that God would honor your desire to know Him and His Word better. Ask God to reveal Himself to you through this process.

THEN, choose a passage of Scripture. Maybe this is a passage you are already studying as part of a Bible reading plan or a small group lesson. If so, that's great. If you don't already have a passage in mind, consider starting with a few verses of Scripture or a smaller passage. If you don't have a passage already chosen, consider choosing one of the following:
- Psalm 3:2-6
- Psalm 27:1
- Psalm 37:4
- Proverbs 3:5-6
- Isaiah 40:31
- Isaiah 41:10
- Zephaniah 3:17
- Matthew 11:28-30
- Romans 8:38-39
- 1 Corinthians 10:13
- Galatians 2:20
- Galatians 5:22-23
- Ephesians 5:1-2
- Philippians 4:8
- Hebrews 4:12
- Hebrews 12:1-2

NEXT, grab a journal, a notebook, a napkin, the back of an envelope, really anything will do, and prepare to write out the passage. Here are a few pointers:
- Start with the Scripture reference. I like to write it first because it helps me remember the passage better for future recall.
- If it is a longer passage, I will write out the verse numbers. I find it helps me remember the passage more clearly when I return to it later.
- Take it slow. This isn't a race. The idea is to let the Word do its work in you while you're so intimately associated with it.
- Finally, write the passage multiple times, especially if it's only one or two verses. See if by the end you can write it without looking at your Bible.

THEN, spend time meditating on the meaning of the passage. What is God trying to show you about Himself? What stands out as significant? How does this passage make you feel? How does it impact your values or your actions?

FINALLY, close in a time of reflective prayer and praise. Thank God for revealing Himself through His Word. Praise Him for who He is.

THE NAMES OF GOD

PART 2

As you find yourself in the third week of this 31-day devotional experience, I want to encourage you to remember what your goal is. Your goal is not just to check a box each day. Your goal is to see your passion for God grow through a very personal, very experiential engagement with the Bible. After all, the Bible is the primary way we can know God. And so our challenge is to see our time in the Word as a meeting with God Himself.

And so, as you did to begin this book a week ago, today you will interact with God using the various ways His character is expressed through His names. Today is looking at descriptive names of God.

For today's challenge, the idea is to choose a name of God that specifically speaks to you based on where you are in your life. Maybe you're in a season when you're facing an uncertain future. Being reminded that God is the "Alpha and the Omega" might be just the thing you need to help you get through the day. Maybe you find yourself hopeful in the midst of new doors God is opening for you. Interacting with God as the "Sun" is a great way to acknowledge Him as the Giver of good things. The idea is to focus on these descriptive names of God as a way of focusing on this specific aspect of who God is.

HERE'S YOUR CHALLENGE FOR TODAY:

FIRST, just as you did on Day 1, set aside a time to read over this list. Pray so that you may get yourself ready to encounter God. Work to free yourself from distractions.

THEN, read through the list a couple of times.

NEXT, choose one of the names of God that speaks to you.

THEN, read the Bible verse where that name is mentioned and reflect on that aspect of who God is.

FINALLY, pray to God using that specific name. Thank God for realizing this role for you. Or, ask Him to help you see Him in this role. Then, offer God praise based on that name. Speak the name back to God. Tell Him who He is. (Again, this is a very biblical practice known as "ascribing.") The idea is for us to deepen our understanding of who God is so that we might experience more of Him in our own lives.

And again, the most important thing is keeping this concept in front of you so that you can constantly reflect on His name.

Bring praise to God today! He is worthy of all our worship.

The Rock
- Read Isaiah 26:4.
- Consider: What about God's strength and permanence speaks to you today?

The Alpha and Omega
- Read Revelation 1:8.
- Consider: God is supreme in all things. He is before all things, and through Him all things have come into being. What "big" challenge or weight in your life looks small in comparison to God?

The Sun
- Read Psalm 84:11.
- Consider: God is the life-giver. He shines His blessings down over us. What good blessing in your life are you particularly thankful for today?

The God Who Sees Me
- Read Genesis 16:13.
- Consider: Praise God that He knows you, hears your prayers, and seeks to meet your needs. What heartfelt need do you need to bring before God today?

The Ancient of Days
- Read Daniel 7:13-14.
- Consider: God is unchanging and He rules all things. How does it impact you knowing that you serve a God so eternally powerful and mighty?

Our Portion
- Read Psalm 73:26.
- Consider: What does it mean to you that God is the only lasting thing in our lives? How does knowing that God is truly all you need help you deal with all that life throws at you?

Our Redeemer
- Read Job 19:25.
- Consider: When all is said and done, God stands as Redeemer. There is nothing that can change the fact that God is the source of your value and worth. How does that make you feel toward God today?

The Helper of the Fatherless
- Read Psalm 10:14.
- Consider: Praise God that He is the perfect Keeper and Provider for us. He sees our grief and knows our trouble. God is ultimately the One who looks after us. Knowing this, how does this change the way that your troubles and worry impact you mentally and emotionally?

The Potter
- Read Isaiah 64:8.
- Consider: God created you personally and lovingly. He continues a good work in you. How are you using your life and your gifts for God's glory?

FINDING JESUS IN PROPHECY

One of the main ideas of this book is that many people struggle with a real, passionate pursuit of God because they aren't properly equipped to look for Him in the Bible. I remember when I was in the Marines. I used to love what the Marines call "land navigation." Given a map, a compass, and grid coordinates, a Marine can get from point A to point B (and points C, D, E, and F if need be) no matter the terrain. Or at least that's the theory.

I was a young Marine and was given an unexpected challenge. Our platoon sergeant looked at me and said, "Blanks, you're leading our patrol tonight." I was a little surprised, but I knew I could handle it. The patrol would be moving 2,000 meters or so through dense woods to meet up with another squad. Not exactly a far patrol, but one in pretty rough terrain. I began plotting our coordinates on my map while the other Marines readied their gear. We set out on the patrol around 10:00 p.m.

Unfortunately, we never met the other squad because we got hopelessly lost. In my first shot at leading a patrol, I forgot a very important piece of information. I won't go into detail because it's too complex to explain here, but there is a process in plotting points on a map where you account for the difference in true north and magnetic north. (See, told you it was complex.) In my excitement of leading this patrol, I skipped this important piece of information. By the time we had traveled a few hundred meters, we were done. The rest of the night was spent with me sheepishly consulting with my squad leaders and trying to navigate by terrain since I had so completely bungled the operation.

I had the will to find our way through the woods; I just wasn't equipped. I believe this describes many Christ-followers, as well. I hope this book changes this.

If we are looking to grow in our hunger for knowing God through His Word, approaching the Bible with an eye toward seeing Christ in all of its pages is a powerful way to do this. And yet, it may not be something many Christ-followers are used to doing. A. W. Tozer, one of my favorite authors, said, "You can be perfectly free to go to your Bible with assurance that you will find Jesus Christ everywhere in its pages." One of the best ways of searching for Jesus in the Bible is by looking at Old Testament prophecies.

I know what you might be thinking. You might not think that searching through Old Testament prophecies is a good way to get you excited about meeting Jesus in the Bible. But this isn't the case. When we prayerfully interact with the many prophecies in Scripture that foretell the details of Jesus' life, we can discover an awe of God's power. More than that, I think it builds an attitude of gratefulness for God's plan; long before we were created, God had set in motion a plan to redeem us from our sins and usher us into God's family.

Today you will spend some time marveling at God's commitment to seek you out. His love is so rich and deep that thousands of years before Christ came to earth, God was laying the foundation for His arrival.

HERE'S YOUR CHALLENGE FOR TODAY:

FIRST, prayerfully prepare your heart to have a time of reflection on God's Word.

THEN, read through each of the prophecies listed below. These are not all of the prophecies concerning Christ, and prophecy isn't the only way to "see" Jesus or the Gospel in the Bible. It is simply a very straightforward way, and so it is the way you will practice today.

Here's a list of some of the Old Testament prophecies concerning Jesus:

Jesus' birth in Bethlehem foretold
Micah 5:2 – "But you, O Bethlehem Ephrathah, who are too little to be among the clans of Judah, from you shall come forth for me one who is to be ruler in Israel, whose coming forth is from of old, from ancient days."

Virgin birth predicted, fulfilled in Mary
Isaiah 7:14 – "Therefore the Lord himself will give you a sign. Behold, the virgin shall conceive and bear a son, and shall call his name Immanuel."

Jesus would be heralded by the messenger of the Lord, fulfilled in John the Baptist
Isaiah 40:3 – "A voice cries: 'In the wilderness prepare the way of the LORD; make straight in the desert a highway for our God.'"

The Holy Spirit would anoint the Messiah, fulfilled most visibly at Christ's baptism
Isaiah 11:2 – "And the Spirit of the LORD shall rest upon him, the Spirit of wisdom and understanding, the Spirit of counsel and might, the Spirit of knowledge and the fear of the LORD."

Jesus' miracles and ministry of healing foretold
Isaiah 35:5-6 – "Then the eyes of the blind shall be opened, and the ears of the deaf unstopped; then shall the lame man leap like a deer, and the tongue of the mute sing for joy. For waters break forth in the wilderness, and streams in the desert."

Jesus' triumphant entry foretold, specifically the part about the donkey (which would have been highly unusual for a King)
Zechariah 9:9 – "Rejoice greatly, O daughter of Zion! Shout aloud, O daughter of Jerusalem! Behold, your king is coming to you; righteous and having salvation is he, humble and mounted on a donkey, on a colt, the foal of a donkey."

Rejected by His people, the Jews
Psalm 118:22 – "The stone that the builders rejected has become the cornerstone."

Jesus' silence before His accusers was foretold
Isaiah 53:7 – "He was oppressed, and he was afflicted, yet he opened not his mouth; like a lamb that is led to the slaughter, and like a sheep that before its shearers is silent, so he opened not his mouth."

Jesus' crucifixion and atonement were foretold
Isaiah 53:5 – "But he was pierced for our transgressions; he was crushed for our iniquities; upon him was the chastisement that brought us peace, and with his wounds we are healed."

Even Jesus' resurrection was foretold
Psalms 16:10 – "For you will not abandon my soul to Sheol, or let your holy one see corruption."

As you read, remind yourself of how each one of these prophecies, written hundreds if not thousands of years before Jesus was born, was fulfilled in Christ. Choose a prophecy that speaks to you and ask yourself the following questions:
- What does this prophecy say to me about God's plan?
- What does this prophecy say to me about God's character?
- What does this prophecy say to me about God's love for me?

FINALLY, let yourself be amazed by God. Let His goodness wash over you. Thank God for His order, His power, His knowledge, and His unfailing, never-ending love. And let these verses help you keep Christ in the forefront of your mind today.

SHHH! THE DISCIPLINE
OF SILENCE

In her work Solitude and Silence, Ruth Haley Barton wrote, "Solitude and silence are not self-indulgent exercises for times when an overcrowded soul needs a little time to itself. Rather, they are concrete ways of opening to the presence of God." Silence. Solitude. I don't know if any two words are more out of place in our world today.

When was the last time you found yourself in a silent environment? And I don't mean an environment that is lacking only sound. I mean an environment free of any stimulus.

No phone. No TV. No laptop. No video games. Nothing. Silence. When was the last time?

I enjoy hunting, and it's easy for me to say that when I hunt, it's silent. This was true when I was a teenager. But now when I hunt, my smartphone is usually in tow with a Kindle book or USA TODAY app just a click away.

True silence is rare. So rare that it is hardly ever found. It has to be provided for. If you want a silent moment, it is usually something only achieved by planning. Nothing about our culture lends itself to silence.

Into this environment, Barton's quote rings true. Silence is a pathway to meeting God. It is today, even in the midst of our fast-paced culture, and it has always been so.

Christ-followers throughout the ages have hidden in monasteries, convents, and retreats, seeking through silence to draw closer to God. Jesus Himself modeled the practice of getting away from the hustle and bustle of His everyday life to commune with God alone and in silence.

"And rising very early in the morning, while it was still dark, he departed and went out to a desolate place, and there he prayed." - Mark 1:35

"But now even more the report about him went abroad, and great crowds gathered to hear him and to be healed of their infirmities. But he would withdraw to desolate places and pray." - Luke 5:15–16

"In these days [Jesus] went out to the mountain to pray, and all night he continued in prayer to God." - Luke 6:12

"And he said to them, 'Come away by yourselves to a desolate place and rest a while.' For many were coming and going, and they had no leisure even to eat. And they went away in the boat to a desolate place by themselves." - Mark 6:31–32

Today's challenge is one of the simplest and yet most difficult ways of engaging with God through the Bible.

Today I would like to encourage you to practice silence.

What does this mean exactly? Am I asking you not to talk at all today? No. Not that kind of silence, though for many of us (me included), less talking and more listening would be a welcomed practice. I want you to find times of silence in your day, pockets when you can turn down any noise or distraction, and use those times to reflect on God.

HERE'S YOUR CHALLENGE FOR TODAY:

FIRST, have these verses available to you today to guide your silence before God. Scripture calls us to the practice of silence. God's Word shows us that silence before God is a good thing and a right response to who God is. Use these verses as a guide to being silent before God.

"But the LORD is in his holy temple; let all the earth keep silence before him." - Habakkuk 2:20

"Be still before the LORD and wait patiently for him . . ." - Psalm 37:7

"Be still, and know that I am God. I will be exalted among the nations, I will be exalted in the earth!" - Psalm 46:10

THEN, deliberately find times of silence in your schedule. On your way to school, don't listen to any music or podcasts. Instead, make time in silence to reflect on and listen to God. Take a walk after school, or close your door this evening and sit in silence. Find a time to spend in reflection and Christ-centered meditation. If it helps, schedule a few periods of silence today using your calendar or timer app on your phone.

In these moments of silence, pray to God, clearing your heart and mind. Pray, and then be still.

Listen.

Meditate.

Reflect.

When something distracting pops up in your head, as it will, push it aside. Refocus.

When you don't know what to do, think about God, but don't force anything.

Feel yourself in God's presence. Feel the Holy Spirit interceding on your behalf.

Just sit. Still. And quiet.

And when you're done, you're done.

Do this three or four times today for at least 15-20 minutes.

Simple. Challenging. And immensely profitable for awakening your desire for God.

DEVOTIONAL READING

PART 2

The older I've gotten, the more I realize the importance of being present. My personality thrives off of action. We have four children who are all active. My wife and I stay busy with our business and ministry pursuits. We are active in our church, and we are social with family and friends. Specifically, because of our busy schedules, family time is extremely valuable to me. While I have not perfectly mastered it, I work hard to make sure that when I'm with my family, I'm 100% there. I am present. I try to limit my interactions with my phone. I work to keep my mind from drifting to deadlines or responsibilities.

Practicing the art of presence is key in making sure I am mentally, physically, and spiritually available to my family. The same is true with your time spent seeking God in His Word.

For today's time of meeting with God, I want to encourage you to practice the devotional reading exercise you first tried in week 1. I chose to have you focus on this again because of your time spent focusing on silent reflection yesterday. Coming out of that exercise, you should be focused. You should be able to approach God through Scripture in a manner in which you are extremely present, focused on God, putting yourself in the position to get the most out of your time with Him.

If you'll recall, I said that this manner of reading the text, "Lectio Divina," is my favorite way of interacting with God in the Bible. It is experiential and heart-focused, and I feel that for me, it opens me up to what God wants to show me through the text. Recall that we said on Day 2 when you last did this exercise that the sole point of devotional reading is to foster a relational, intimate interaction with God through the Bible. It asks the question, "What does God want to show me in this text?"

As you prepare to practice devotional reading today, remember that the ability to listen to the passage is an important aspect of this practice. I prefer reading the passage aloud. But you can also listen to it on a Bible app (such as YouVersion) or through a website (like Biblegateway.com).

HERE'S A REMINDER OF HOW IT WORKS:

FIRST, find somewhere quiet. Quiet your mind. Prepare your heart. Slow down. Get yourself ready to meet God in His Word. Start with a prayer to God, asking Him to reveal to you what He has for you in this passage.

THEN, read Psalm 119:9-16 below, or choose your own passage. Read it slowly and out loud. By slowly, I mean almost word by word. The idea is to read as if God is going to stop you and show you something at any moment. As you come across words or phrases that seem to speak to you, pause and focus on them. Think about what it is about them that speaks to you. But most of all, listen to what the Spirit is trying to show you. Here's the passage:

> "[9] How can a young man keep his way pure? By guarding it according to your word. [10] With my whole heart I seek you; let me not wander from your commandments! [11] I have stored up your word in my heart, that I might not sin against you. [12] Blessed are you, O LORD; teach me your statutes! [13] With my lips I declare all the rules of your mouth. [14] In the way of your testimonies I delight as much as in all riches. [15] I will meditate on your precepts and fix my eyes on your ways. [16] I will delight in your statutes; I will not forget your word." - Psalm 119:9-16

NEXT, contemplate the passage even deeper by reading it aloud one more time. This time, really soak in the words and ideas you're encountering. If God wants you to think on certain principles, do so. Allow the words to guide your interaction with God. If you need some prompts to guide your devotion, consider some of the following questions:

- · How does my emotional engagement with God's Word compare to the author's? For example, can I say that I truly seek God with all my heart? Do I rejoice in knowing and obeying God?

- · What needs to happen for me to have the same emotional longing for knowing God through His Word?

- · How would other areas of my life be impacted if my desire for God and His Word increased?

THEN, you need to consider your response. This is your chance to engage in a conversation with God. Pray to Him, asking Him what He wants to show you. Express to Him how the truths He led you to reflect on made you feel.

FINALLY, summarize to yourself what you have learned. Some people like to jot these thoughts down in a journal. Some can do this mentally. But the idea is to spend some time – however much you spend is up to you – just thinking about what God has shown you and how it changes who you are. Try to hone in on specific concepts that you can take away.

CONVICTION, CONFESSION, REPENTANCE

Part of being human means accepting that we really, really don't like it when things are difficult or painful. It's why exercise can be both super-awful and yet so good for us. I have been a runner since I was a teenager. Not a particularly good one, mind you, but a runner nonetheless. I enjoy running long-distance races, especially trail races, because of the mental toughness it takes and teaches. Running an ultra trail race is more about mentally being able to run through pain to accomplish your goal. A friend of mine is an Ironman finisher and an accomplished triathlete. He once told me that to excel as a long-distance runner, "you must become comfortable with discomfort." This is so true, and yet really hard for us to accept.

We tend to avoid discomfort in our lives, and mostly, it serves us well. However, this same practice in our spiritual lives can actually hurt us.

Throughout Scripture, we see people modeling what we may call the "sin/confession/repentance" cycle. This is where a person (or people) is made aware of their sin, confesses it to God, and commits to turning from this sin. We see this in the lives of God's people, the Israelites. We see this in King Saul. We see this in David. And we see it commanded as a pattern in the New Testament.

When we are made aware of our sin, the right thing to do in God's eyes is to confess the sin and set your will against doing it any longer. Now, because we are sinful at heart, we know we will never be sinless this side of heaven. But there is something powerful in this pattern, or else God wouldn't have commanded it.

What does this practice have to do with awakening your passion for God and for encountering Him in His Word? Plenty. The concepts of sin and mercy are at the heart of what it means to be a Christ-follower. Sin is defined as falling short of God's standards. Because of this, we have to know God to truly understand our sin. (If we don't know what God expects of us, how can we know if we've fallen short?) And forgiveness from sin is something God alone can offer us. Repentance is merely us doing all that we can do as finite, fallible humans to obey a perfect God.

This cycle is really important to our understanding of who God is and our relationship with Him. However, few of us practice it because it is discomforting. It is painful. It is humiliating (in the best kind of way). However, by not practicing confession and repentance, we are failing to experience the richness of our relationship with God.

Today you will use God's Word to engage in a time of conviction, confession, and repentance. You will see that there is not a lot of content provided for you. The meat of your time today will be spent in quiet, humble submission in prayer before God.

Confession is not always comfortable. It's not always easy. But experiencing the assurance of God's love and forgiveness is worth the discomfort we experience when we face our sins before God. Embrace this time today. Lean on the grace and mercy of God.

HERE'S YOUR CHALLENGE FOR TODAY:

FIRST, read Psalm 25:8. Meditate on God's goodness.
- "Good and upright is the LORD; therefore he instructs sinners in the way."
  - Psalm 25:8

THEN, read Psalm 32:5. Confess any sins or sin habits to God.
- "I acknowledged my sin to you, and I did not cover my iniquity; I said, 'I will confess my transgressions to the LORD,' and you forgave the iniquity of my sin." - Psalm 32:5

NEXT, accept the forgiveness that God offers through faith in His Son, Jesus. Reflect on what this means to you. Thank God for His plan of extending salvation to you.
- "If we confess our sins, he is faithful and just to forgive us our sins and to cleanse us from all unrighteousness." – 1 John 1:9

THEN, express to God your desire to repent from your sin, asking the Holy Spirit to empower you to turn away from areas you need to turn away from.
- "The Lord is not slow to fulfill his promise as some count slowness, but is patient toward you, not wishing that any should perish, but that all should reach repentance." – 2 Peter 3:9

FINALLY, read Psalm 32:1. Thank God for His willingness to forgive you and His desire to make you righteous. As much as possible, meditate on this final verse today.
- "Blessed is the one whose transgression is forgiven, whose sin is covered."
  - Psalm 32:1

USING YOUR IMAGINATION

The Bible is one really long story made up of lots of individual stories. Lots and lots of stories. But the way that some of these stories are told doesn't always have the kinds of descriptive details you encounter when you read a novel or any other kind of narrative. That's because the purpose of the biblical authors isn't the same as the purpose of your favorite novelist.

John, who is as descriptive a writer as you'll find in the Bible, wasn't necessarily concerned that we knew what the wine smelled like at the wedding feast at Cana, or how the festivities sounded, or the color of the groom's coat. In relaying the story of Jesus' first miracle, John was most concerned with narrating a true story as a way of proving Jesus' identity as the Son of God. Period. Because this was his purpose, there were descriptive details he left out.

I'm a big-time reader. I'm reading multiple books at once at all times. I've been this way since I was your age. Among other things, I like to read military history. I love it when an author paints vivid descriptions of the sights, smells, and sounds of a battle. I can almost put myself in the action. We don't always get the same vivid descriptions of biblical narratives because it simply wasn't the authors' intent, nor is it an aspect of the Scripture that we should always come to expect. While this is true, and while it doesn't take away anything from the stories we encounter in the Bible, it does create a barrier of sorts for us at times.

We have a problem when we read the Bible, especially the many wonderful narrative passages. We often read these passages as one dimensional, rather cold descriptions of events. We rarely, if ever, stop to think about what it was like to be IN the story or that the accounts we read were actual, historical events that happened within the rich sensory context that real life happens in.

When Jesus was talking to the Samaritan woman at the well in John 4, have you ever considered what the weather was like? Was it windy? Was it an overcast day or was the sun beating down on them?

What did the woman look like? What were her mannerisms like as Jesus engaged her in such a thrilling conversation? What did she sound like? Was her voice small and timid? Or was she bold?

What did the disciples' faces look like as they approached Jesus at the end of the conversation? How did it sound when they walked up to Jesus, sandals shuffling in the sands of Samaria?

When the woman ran back and shared the story of her remarkable interaction with Jesus, what did those conversations look like? Was she out of breath? Was she weeping? How did the townspeople look in response?

As people seeking to awaken our passion for God and for meeting Him in His Word, one of the ways we do this is by embracing our imagination when it comes to reading the powerful narratives of the Bible.

Do you ever engage your imagination when you read Scripture? Do you ever take the time to mentally place yourself in the story and look around you to see it come alive? It's an interesting practice, one that comes more easily to some than others, but one that can help you draw closer to God by seeing the Bible come alive in ways that maybe it hasn't to you before.

I remember the first time I was exposed to this way of interacting with God and His Word. A friend of mine who is an excellent and very creative Bible communicator lead us in this exercise. When I first heard it described, I was skeptical. And I believe the reason I was skeptical still serves as a fair warning for us as we think about this method of engaging with Scripture.

My skepticism centered on the concern that even though our imaginations are focused on events described in the Bible, they can't be taken as having the same weight as Scripture. God's Word is perfect. We aren't. And therefore, our imaginations aren't. Taken to the extreme, this practice could lead you to consider what you imagine in a way that could lead you to an interpretation or understanding of the Bible that is outside of the absolute truth of Scripture. And yet, even with this warning as a backdrop, I believe that for many people, this practice helps bring Scripture to life.

If this practice sounds like something that could help you awaken your joy for God's Word, then embrace it. Just know that it's only a tool to help you better interact with Scripture, not a replacement on equal footing with the inspired Word of God.

HERE'S YOUR CHALLENGE FOR TODAY:

FIRST, turn to your favorite Gospel. Then, find a narrative passage where Jesus is preaching, performing a miracle, or healing.

THEN, carefully read the passage one time through to familiarize yourself with it.

NEXT, re-read the passage while paying close attention to any sensory clues or descriptions of the context in which the story takes place.

THEN, close your eyes. Use your imagination to picture what the setting looks like. Imagine the sounds you hear as you put yourself in that place. Imagine what the air feels like. Does the story allow you room to imagine any particular smells? Imagine you're looking around you. Who is there? What do they look like?

As you imagine the scenario, glance back at the text. Read Jesus' words or the descriptions of His actions. Imagine Jesus speaking or acting in the scene you have set in your mind. Hear His voice. See Him speaking. Imagine others interacting with Jesus. Imagine what your reaction would be if you were actually in the story as you have pictured it in your mind.

FINALLY, spend some time in prayer, talking to God, and listening to what He has to tell you. Thank God that He gave us His Word so that we would have a record of His interaction with us, His people. Praise Him that He chooses to make Himself known to us.

FOCUSING ON THE PROMISES
OF GOD

PART 2

Let's drop our guard for a moment. If we're honest, we'd admit that while life is full of a lot of really fun things, it has its share of stuff that's a real bummer. Sometimes school is a life-drainer. Sometimes we face major issues with our family. Sometimes, no matter how well we think we're doing with our friends, we find ourselves in the middle of relationship drama. Sometimes we struggle with depression, anxiety, or despair. Sometimes we look around us and wonder how we got here.

If you feel this way at times, you're not a bad Christian. You're not any more broken than anyone else. You're not weird. Or alone. If you feel this way, it simply means that you're human.

Tough times are part of what it means to be human. They weren't supposed to be originally. God created Eden to be a place of perfection, where man and woman and their kids could walk with their Creator in perfect relational harmony. But sin destroyed this peace. As a result, creation (including humans) has been broken ever since. There are beautiful days when little sparks of God shine through, and there are rough days when a frustrated creation seems to rule. On these days, God's promises are more vital than ever to our well-being.

This is another day of focusing on the promises of God. If you skipped the first devotional in which we focused on God's promises, or you need a refresher, I would strongly encourage you to review some of the cautions I mentioned in Day 6. We must approach God's promises carefully, but we should also approach them hopefully.

In God's promises, we see His heart for His people. As we seek to rediscover, or discover for the first time, a meaningful connection with God through His Word, counting on God's promises connects us to the heart of a Father who hears the cries of His children and commits to meeting the needs of their souls. God is perfectly and eternally faithful and good. He is incapable of NOT keeping a promise, either in this world or the next.

Make time today to seek out the comfort His promises hold for His children.

HERE'S YOUR CHALLENGE FOR TODAY:

FIRST, read the list of promises below and the accompanying Scripture:

God promises peace when we are anxious.
"Do not be anxious about anything, but in everything by prayer and supplication with thanksgiving let your requests be made known to God. And the peace of God, which surpasses all understanding, will guard your hearts and your minds in Christ Jesus." - Philippians 4:6-7

God promises to guide us when we need direction.
"Trust in the LORD with all your heart, and do not lean on your own understanding. In all your ways acknowledge him, and he will make straight your paths." - Proverbs 3:5-6

God promises rest for our souls.
"Come to me, all who labor and are heavy laden, and I will give you rest. Take my yoke upon you, and learn from me, for I am gentle and lowly in heart, and you will find rest for your souls. For my yoke is easy, and my burden is light." - Matthew 11:28-30

God promises to one day gather His children to Himself.
"In my Father's house are many rooms. If it were not so, would I have told you that I go to prepare a place for you? And if I go and prepare a place for you, I will come again and will take you to myself, that where I am you may be also." - John 14:2-3

God promises to forgive our sins if we confess them to Him.
"If we confess our sins, he is faithful and just to forgive us our sins and to cleanse us from all unrighteousness." - 1 John 1:9

God promises comfort in times of trial.
"Even though I walk through the valley of the shadow of death, I will fear no evil, for you are with me; your rod and your staff, they comfort me." - Psalm 23:4

God promises to meet our needs.

"Therefore do not be anxious, saying, 'What shall we eat?' or 'What shall we drink?' or 'What shall we wear?' For the Gentiles seek after all these things, and your heavenly Father knows that you need them all. But seek first the kingdom of God and his righteousness, and all these things will be added to you." - Matthew 6:31–33

God promises that one day, He will bring an end to pain, suffering, and death.

"He will wipe away every tear from their eyes, and death shall be no more, neither shall there be mourning, nor crying, nor pain anymore, for the former things have passed away." - Revelation 21:4

God promises His presence when we turn to Him in our despair.

"The LORD is a stronghold for the oppressed, a stronghold in times of trouble. And those who know your name put their trust in you, for you, O LORD, have not forsaken those who seek you." - Psalm 9:9–10

THEN, find the one promise that speaks to where you are in your life right now. What promise leaps off the page at you? What situation do you find yourself in where you need God to show up in a specific way? Identify the promise above that is most relevant to your life today.

NEXT, think about how specifically the promise you've chosen impacts your situation. How does it make you feel? What does the promise offer you? How does this promise change the way you think about where you find yourself? What might be some of the possible ways, considering your situation, in which God keeps His promise?

THEN, spend some focused time in prayer, bringing both God's promise and your specific situation before God. Thank God for His faithfulness and His sovereignty. Tell God that you trust Him to keep His promise even though you may not get to see or understand how exactly He does it. Confess to God your belief in His perfect will and tell Him that you know He will fulfill His promise to you in a way that is in line with His character.

FINALLY, memorize the verses that contain the promise you've chosen. Keep them in front of you today and in the future. Look for how God will answer your promise. Expect Him to! And be ready to acknowledge Him in praise and thankfulness when He does.

THE DOING OF GOD'S WORD

At the ministry I co-founded, youthministry360, we have seven value statements that serve as a map for our organization. They are on creative posters throughout our building. We focus on them in our weekly staff meetings. Several relate to how we treat our customers, and it's not uncommon to hear a team member acknowledge the efforts of another team member by speaking one of our values to them ("Way to crush that hassle!"). For our ministry, our values aren't just a page in an employee handbook. We strive to see them lived out in our culture.

I have noticed over the years that most organizations have value statements, but many of them aren't put to use. They are often just window dressing for the lobby or the conference room. I've often wondered if you stopped someone at one of these businesses how well could they recite their company's values or mission statement.

We must be careful that the same can't be said about our faith.

Much of what you have been challenged to do in this book affects what we might call the head and the heart. As we have worked to awaken our passion for God and the Bible, we've addressed our emotions and our values (heart), as well as how we think about our God and His role in our lives (head). In today's devotion, I want us to focus not on our heads or our hearts, but on our hands.

Our faith put to action is one of the main themes of the Bible, particularly the New Testament. It's impossible to be a Christian and to know the ways of God but not see the ways of God lived out in your life. James, the brother of Jesus and leader of the Jerusalem church, said it best:

> "[14] What good is it, my brothers, if someone says he has faith but does not have works? Can that faith save him? [15] If a brother or sister is poorly clothed and lacking in daily food, [16] and one of you says to them, 'Go in peace, be warmed and filled,' without giving them the things needed for the body, what good is that? [17] So also faith by itself, if it does not have works, is dead." - James 2:14-17

James asks an interesting question: Can a faith that doesn't result in any righteous actions really be described as faith? As we know, we're not saved by our actions. We're saved by faith in Jesus. But our Christlike deeds are the proof of our salvation. James, who was kind of big on this concept, said it another way in James 1:22: "But be doers of the word, and not hearers only, deceiving yourselves." The prophet Micah put it this way in Micah 6:8: "He has told you, O man, what is good; and what does the LORD require of you but to do justice, and to love kindness, and to walk humbly with your God?" These are just a few of the hundreds of moments in Scripture when the people of God are commanded to act like the people of God.

Today's devotion is another that challenges you to allow the time you spend in the Word to spill over into your daily life. The goal for today is to be motivated by the heart of God as expressed in the Word of God to act like a child of God. Do something today that is unmistakably Christlike and motivated by your identity as a Christian. And do it in the name of Christ. Anyone can do something nice for someone. Your challenge today is to serve someone for their good and God's glory.

HERE'S YOUR CHALLENGE FOR TODAY:

FIRST, read through the verses below that speak to God's desire that we would be people whose lives reflect the heart of our Father, especially as it relates to the poor or the outcast. Choose a verse that speaks to you the most. Use it for your motivation today. If you're feeling extra awesome, consider memorizing it.

> "[7] If among you, one of your brothers should become poor, in any of your towns within your land that the LORD your God is giving you, you shall not harden your heart or shut your hand against your poor brother, [8] but you shall open your hand to him and lend him sufficient for his need, whatever it may be." - Deuteronomy 15:7–8

> "Whoever is generous to the poor lends to the LORD, and he will repay him for his deed." - Proverbs 19:17

> "If you pour yourself out for the hungry and satisfy the desire of the afflicted, then shall your light rise in the darkness and your gloom be as the noonday." - Isaiah 58:10

> "He has told you, O man, what is good; and what does the LORD require of you but to do justice, and to love kindness, and to walk humbly with your God?" - Micah 6:8

"Give to the one who begs from you, and do not refuse the one who would borrow from you." - Matthew 5:42

"[34] Then the King will say to those on his right, 'Come, you who are blessed by my Father, inherit the kingdom prepared for you from the foundation of the world. [35] For I was hungry and you gave me food, I was thirsty and you gave me drink, I was a stranger and you welcomed me, [36] I was naked and you clothed me, I was sick and you visited me, I was in prison and you came to me.' [37] Then the righteous will answer him, saying, 'Lord, when did we see you hungry and feed you, or thirsty and give you drink? [38] And when did we see you a stranger and welcome you, or naked and clothe you? [39] And when did we see you sick or in prison and visit you?' [40] And the King will answer them, 'Truly, I say to you, as you did it to one of the least of these my brothers, you did it to me.'" - Matthew 25:34–40

"Give, and it will be given to you. Good measure, pressed down, shaken together, running over, will be put into your lap. For with the measure you use it will be measured back to you." - Luke 6:38

"[6] The point is this: whoever sows sparingly will also reap sparingly, and whoever sows bountifully will also reap bountifully. [7] Each one must give as he has decided in his heart, not reluctantly or under compulsion, for God loves a cheerful giver." - 2 Corinthians 9:6-7

"They are to do good, to be rich in good works, to be generous and ready to share." - 1 Timothy 6:18

"Do not neglect to do good and to share what you have, for such sacrifices are pleasing to God." – Hebrews 13:16

"[16] By this we know love, that he laid down his life for us, and we ought to lay down our lives for the brothers. [17] But if anyone has the world's goods and sees his brother in need, yet closes his heart against him, how does God's love abide in him? [18] Little children, let us not love in word or talk but in deed and in truth." - 1 John 3:16–18

THEN, make it a point in the next day or so to invest yourself in an act of service. Really give this some careful thought. I don't mean simply being kind to the lady behind the counter at Target (though, that is a super cool thing to do and you should do it all the time regardless) or buying the coffee for the person behind you in line at Starbucks (again, a very nice thing to do). I want to challenge you to do something in the next couple of days that is intentional, and that is relational beyond just exchanging pleasantries. Something that requires sacrifice on your part, and that is done in a way that connects your good deed with the Gospel.

It's easy for us to do nice things for others without connecting our actions with our faith. And there is nothing wrong with that at all. But for this particular challenge, I want you to make sure you let the recipient of your act of service know that you are motivated to serve them because of your faith in God.

Here's the deal: this is a very easy challenge for you to skip over. If you have a strong faith life and are walking closely with the Lord, you may be tempted to see this as a devotion that doesn't apply to you. If you're in a season when you are not as close to God as you want to be, you may feel like this is just another task. It may feel a bit hollow. Regardless of where you find yourself, I want to encourage you to follow through with what this devotion has suggested. Why? Because we are never closer to the heart of God than when we are pouring ourselves out sacrificially for the good of others in the name of God. Draw closer to God today by being the hands and feet of Christ to someone who needs God's presence in their lives.

DAY

TWENTY-SEVEN

LEARNING FROM THE CHARACTERS OF THE BIBLE

PART 2

Have you ever been around people who seem to have a special connection with God? They radiate God's character. In their words and actions, you can tell they routinely spend time in God's presence. When I'm around these people, I leave feeling encouraged and inspired. I find myself wanting what they have. I want MORE of God!

Believe it or not, we can experience the same effect by spending time with the characters we meet in Scripture. We can be encouraged and empowered by learning from people who had unique relationships with God.

This is the second of two devotions where we look at some key biblical characters. (However, you could mine weeks of Bible Study from the two lists of characters that appear in this book.) We're not going to do anything much different in this look at characters from Scripture. The goal is to see a spark in these characters that lights a spark in you.

If you want more from your relationship with God, if you have a feeling that the nature of your faith should be more alive, spend some time asking yourself what you can learn from the people who make up the list below. What from their life speaks to you? What about their example helps you wake up to a passionate pursuit of God?

Enjoy this second encounter with these awesome saints of old.

HERE'S YOUR CHALLENGE FOR TODAY:

FIRST, prayerfully read the list of people below. If you chose a favorite character last time you did this, you might want to choose a character you aren't as familiar with this time (and vice versa). Whichever direction you choose to take, select a character from the list below:

Adam - First person created. Enjoyed a personal relationship with God in the Garden of Eden before his sin caused God to send him out.
- Main Passage: Genesis 1:26-5:5
- Other Places: Luke 3:38; Romans 5:14; 1 Corinthians 15:22, 45; 1 Timothy 2:13-14

Daniel - Taken captive when Babylon conquered Israel. Faithful to God. Had an interesting encounter with a bunch of lions.
- Main Passage: Book of Daniel

David - Shepherd boy turned mighty king. God called David a man after His own heart. Wrote most of the Psalms.
- Main Passages: 1 Samuel 16-1; Kings 2
- Other Places: Matthew 1:1-6, 22:43-45; Luke 1:32; Acts 13:22; Romans 1:3; Hebrews 11:32

Eve – Second person created. Also enjoyed a personal relationship with God in the Garden before her sin drove her away.
- Main Passage: Genesis 2:18-4:26

Isaac - Son of the covenant born to Abraham and Sarah. Father to Jacob and Esau.
- Main Passage: Genesis 17:15-35:29
- Other Places: Romans 9:7-10; Hebrews 11:17-20; James 2:21

Jacob - Grandson of Abraham. Son of Isaac. Father of the 12 Tribes of Israel. Flawed, but still used by God.
- Main Passage: Genesis 25-50
- Other Places: Matthew 1:2, 22:32; Acts 7:8-16; Romans 9:11-13; Hebrews 11:9, 20-21

Jonah - Prophet who got it wrong a lot more than he got it right. Fish expert.
- Main Passage: Book of Jonah
- Other Places: Matthew 12:39-41; Luke 11:32

Joseph - Amazing story: sold into slavery by his brothers. Falsely imprisoned. Became a great Egyptian ruler.
- Main Passage: Genesis 30-50
- Other Places: Hebrews 11:22

Mary, Mother of Jesus - Jesus' virgin mother. God miraculously formed Jesus in her womb.
- Main Passages: Luke 1:26-56, 2:1-20; Matthew 1:18-25
- Other Places: John 2:1-12; Acts 1:14

Paul - Outside of Christ, most influential person for Christianity. Converted persecutor of Christ-followers. Wrote 13 New Testament books.
- Main Passage: Acts 7:58-28:31
- Other Places: Choose one of Paul's letters (his letters to Timothy and the Philippians are particularly revealing of his character)

Philip - One of the seven men that helped the apostles minister to the needy in the early Church. Ministered throughout Samaria. Baptized the Ethiopian official.
- Main Passages: Acts 6:1-7, 8:4-8
- Other Places: Acts 8:26-40

Rahab - Prostitute who came to believe in God. Rescued Joshua and Caleb. Included in Jesus' lineage.
- Main Passages: Joshua 2, 6:22-23
- Other Places: Matthew 1:5; Hebrews 11:31; James 2:25

Timothy - Mentored by Paul. Young pastor and leader in the New Testament Church. Recipient of Paul's letters 1 and 2 Timothy.
- Main Passage: Acts 16
- Other Places: 1 Corinthians 4:17, 16:10-11; Philippians 2:19-23; 1 Thessalonians 3:2-6; Hebrews 13:23

THEN, taking advantage of a journal or a note-taking app, begin to read about your character's life, writing down the noteworthy details that stand out to you. Like last time, some of the characters above have stories that are longer than others. Whether it's a long story or a relatively short one, read the story of the character you have chosen.

NEXT, when you have finished, ask yourself the same questions that were asked the last time you did this exercise.
- What did I learn about God in this story? How do I see God interacting with this person? Where do I see God's sovereign plan shine through in this person's life?

- What did I learn about the specific person? What positive traits did they show? What kind of person do they seem to be? What, if any, weaknesses revealed themselves? How did they approach God?

- What can I learn about myself? Where do I see lessons to be applied to my own faith life? How would I react if put in the place of the character? What about this person's story exposes something in me that needs to change or be strengthened?

Just like last time, when you've finished, spend some time in prayer, listening to what God has to say to you and thanking Him that He is a loving God that cares so deeply about His people.

FINALLY, use this question as the guide for helping you continue to think about your character as you go through the next few days:
God, what are you trying to show me about my life through this character's story?

Ask this question over a few days. Listen to what God is telling you. God is faithful and will reveal to you what He wants you to know about Him and you.

WHAT IT MEANS TO BE EXPECTANT

Think about the big events of your life. Birthdays. Graduations. Awards banquets. The first day of vacation. Holidays. The one thing that makes these types of moments so meaningful is the buildup. Think about it: Christmas is such a significant season because of the anticipation. (That's what Advent is all about.) The preparation for the big day, whatever it is, makes the big day even that more meaningful.

It doesn't even have to be a significant life event. I love music. Part of the fun of a concert is the days leading up to it, listening to the music of the artist you're going to see, wondering what the setlist will be, what songs they'll play for the encore, and so on. Heck, I get excited when my wife tells me we're going to our favorite restaurant. The excitement adds to the experience.

Have you ever thought whether your sense of expectancy, or lack thereof, impacts the way you experience God?

Here's the deal: God moves all around us all the time. It's been true since He first spoke creation into being. God has always been active in our everyday world. It is a theological truth (sometimes called "God's immanence"). If this is true, why don't we notice it more? If it is true that God is at work around us, and if it is also true that we don't often or ever recognize this work, it must be that the problem is with us.

We have an expectancy problem. Most of us don't look for God to move and, therefore, we don't see Him move.

Let's look at a very simple example of this. Have you ever asked God for something in prayer and then found that you were surprised when He answered you? I'll be honest with you and share that I have done this very thing. We ask God not really believing that He will answer. This is significant because the Bible, the actual book God gave us so that we would know Him, is full of evidence that God is an active God who works all around us all the time answering our prayers and acting for His glory and our good. And we are caught off guard at times by God acting perfectly in line with His character.

Think about the prophets of the Old Testament. Think about the Israelites. Think about the leaders of Israel, from the judges to David and Solomon. Think about the disciples. Think about Paul. Every single one of these people lived in full assurance that God was not only able to move in their midst, but that at any moment it was going to happen. They relied on it. They counted on it. And they were right.

In case you haven't noticed by now, there have been a few days scattered throughout this book when you have been challenged to do something that goes beyond your time of engaging with Scripture. These have been more practical. On Day 7, you were challenged to fast from food. On Day 14, you were challenged to fast from media. On Day 21, you were challenged to practice silence. Today, you're going to be challenged to do something that is at its outset seemingly abstract. Today, I want to challenge you to practice expectancy. (See? Told you it would sound abstract.) How do we do this?

HERE'S YOUR CHALLENGE FOR TODAY:

FIRST, take a moment and see where we encounter this attitude in Scripture. The Bible has much to say about expectancy. The language the Bible uses to describe this attitude is "waiting on the Lord." What a beautiful picture! As we would wait for an appointment with a friend, a family member, or a youth minister, we wait on God. Read through the following verses. Choose one or two that stand out to you. Prayerfully meditate on these verses, internalizing their truth.

> "I wait for the LORD, my soul waits, and in his word I hope; my soul waits for the Lord more than watchmen for the morning, more than watchmen for the morning." - Psalm 130:5-6

> "My God in his steadfast love will meet me; God will let me look in triumph on my enemies." - Psalm 59:10

> "For God alone, O my soul, wait in silence, for my hope is from him." - Psalm 62:5

> "O LORD, be gracious to us; we wait for you. Be our arm every morning, our salvation in the time of trouble." - Isaiah 33:2

> "From of old no one has heard or perceived by the ear, no eye has seen a God besides you, who acts for those who wait for him." - Isaiah 64:4

"The Lord is good to those who wait for him, to the soul who seeks him."
- Lamentations 3:25

"But as for me, I will look to the LORD; I will wait for the God of my salvation; my God will hear me." - Micah 7:7

THEN, spend some time in prayer. If you know that, like many of us, you are guilty of not living your life expecting to see God work in and through you each day, confess this to God. Confess to God why you think this is. Ask God in prayer to work through His Holy Spirit to bring about change in your life. Ask the Spirit to work in you to open your eyes to what God is doing in the world around you. Praise God that He chooses to lovingly reveal His works to us, His children.

NEXT, practice expectancy. Ha! Sounds simple enough, doesn't it? The truth is that it actually is. As you go through the next few days, be mindful of any interaction or circumstance in which you encounter something that is a result of God at work. It could be as simple as being moved by a particularly beautiful sunset or as deep as God answering a long-time prayer. Remember, God is moving all around us all the time. We don't often see it because we don't look for it. Look for God. Expect to see Him moving as if it is an inevitability, as if you would be surprised if you didn't. That is what practicing expectancy is all about.

FINALLY, consider recording these encounters with God in a journal or note-taking app. One of the key principles in having a passionate relationship with God is remembering what He has done for you in your life. Spending a few days tracking the ways you see God at work is a valuable way of awakening your joy for God.

THE NAMES OF GOD

PART 3

The presence of God in our lives is a powerful thing. My prayer for you is that by this point in this book, you have sensed God's presence more. The truth about God is that He is never far away.

There are seasons in our lives when this truth doesn't feel true. These can be dry, dark days. How refreshing it is to be reminded that God is deeply engaged in impacting the lives of His children!

If you've gone through this book in order, you're just about to wrap up the month-long journey of awakening your passion for God. I'd like to strongly encourage you to come at these last few days with a fresh heart and a renewed mind, seeking to draw closer to God through daily interactions with Him through His Word.

Today, as we've done twice already, we're going to meet God in His Word through looking at (more of) His names. (How awesome is it that there are still more names of God for us to look at?) However, today I want to do this a little differently than we have before.

As Christ-followers, we are called to make much of others' needs. As we journey to awaken our passion for God, it may be easy to focus only on our spiritual needs. There are people around us, people whom we are close with and others whom we only know tangentially, who also need to be awakened to God's presence in their lives.

Today we are going to encounter God through the Scriptures in a familiar way, but we're going to do so with an external focus. We're not going to consider our own needs today, but the needs of other people in our lives.

HERE'S YOUR CHALLENGE FOR TODAY:

FIRST, I want to encourage you to prayerfully read through the following names of God, thoughtfully focusing on each one and what they mean.

Our Fortress
"But I will sing of your strength; I will sing aloud of your steadfast love in the morning. For you have been to me a fortress and a refuge in the day of my distress." - Psalm 59:16

The Light of the World
"Again Jesus spoke to them, saying, 'I am the light of the world. Whoever follows me will not walk in darkness, but will have the light of life.'" - John 8:12

The Counselor
"But the Helper, the Holy Spirit, whom the Father will send in my name, he will teach you all things and bring to your remembrance all that I have said to you." - John 14:26

Our Refuge
"Because you have made the LORD your dwelling place—the Most High, who is my refuge—no evil shall be allowed to befall you, no plague come near your tent." - Psalm 91:9–10

The Bright Morning Star
"'I, Jesus, have sent my angel to testify to you about these things for the churches. I am the root and the descendant of David, the bright morning star.'" - Revelation 22:16

Our Deliverer
"As for me, I am poor and needy, but the Lord takes thought for me. You are my help and my deliverer; do not delay, O my God!" - Psalm 40:17

The Prince of Peace
"For to us a child is born, to us a son is given; and the government shall be upon his shoulder, and his name shall be called Wonderful Counselor, Mighty God, Everlasting Father, Prince of Peace." - Isaiah 9:6

THEN, I want you to think of one person in your life who truly needs to experience this particular aspect of God's character in their lives. (For example, maybe you are thinking of someone who is in the midst of a tough time apart from God. Maybe for this person, you would pray that God would impact his or her life as the "Light of the World," revealing Himself to this person and leading him or her out of darkness and into light.)

NEXT, spend time meditating on this aspect of God's character, praying that God would make Himself known in this person's life in this way. Pray that God's character would illuminate this person's world, drawing them closer to Him in a profound way. Trust God that He can and will reveal Himself to this individual in His perfect timing.

FINALLY, carry this image of God with you today, reflecting on a God who pursues us and longs to engage with us according to His character.

ENGAGING WITH GOD'S WORD
THROUGH SONG

I love music. I mean, I really love it. I have since I was a child. My parents loved music, and I grew up in a house where there was always music being played. My brothers were both musically inclined, playing multiple instruments well. I got none of that talent, but I still love music of all kinds. Americana, jazz, rock, hip-hop, rock, pop, classical . . . There are very few genres I don't like. If you follow me on Instagram or Facebook, you'll see lots of images from concerts, many of which I have dragged my lovely wife to (who likes music but maybe doesn't share my exact passion for it). I love that my children share my love for music because that means more music for me to listen to!

Did you know that when God created people, He birthed in us a desire to engage Him through song? According to Scripture, music is actually a VERY important part of our relationship with God. And music is a powerful tool for us to focus on as we seek to be people with a passion for God and His Word.

When we think of music and Scripture, our minds automatically go to the Psalms, and for good reason. So many of the Psalms, whether penned by David or other authors, were created as songs. (The word psalms comes from the Greek word "to sing.") You can't go far in the Psalms without encountering the concept of engaging with God through song:

> "My lips will shout for joy, when I sing praises to you; my soul also, which you have redeemed." - Psalm 71:23

> "Oh come, let us sing to the LORD; let us make a joyful noise to the rock of our salvation!" - Psalm 95:1

> "Praise the LORD, for the LORD is good; sing to his name, for it is pleasant!" - Psalm 135:3

The command to reach out to God in song isn't limited just to the Psalms or even to the Old Testament. The Apostle Paul understood the importance music plays in our relationship with God. In Ephesians 5:19, he encouraged the Ephesian Christ-followers to "[address] one another in psalms and hymns and spiritual songs, singing and making melody to the Lord with your heart." Again, in his letter to the Colossians he expressed similar sentiments, encouraging the Christians at Colossae to "let the word of Christ dwell in you richly, teaching and admonishing one another in all wisdom, singing psalms and hymns and spiritual songs, with thankfulness in your hearts to God" (Col. 3:16). I love the direct connection Paul makes here to God's Word and song.

When the Bible talks about us coming to a saving relationship with God, He is said to "put a new song in my mouth, a song of praise" (Ps. 40:3). When we join God in heaven for eternity, this "new song" is echoed again: "and they were singing a new song before the throne" (Rev. 14:3). Music is like a thread woven through our lives as Christ-followers. It's an important part of connecting and interacting with God.

Now, surely there are some of you saying, "Andy, this sounds great, but music just isn't my thing." Certainly, we fall on various points across a spectrum; for some, music and singing is more of a primary way of connecting with God. For others, it's something they experience primarily as a part of corporate worship with their local congregation, but not a big part of their everyday lives. Regardless of where you fall on this spectrum, you were designed by God to lift your voice to Him in song. To neglect it is to neglect a part of your identity.

For today's devotional experience, I want to help you meet with God in song. I want to do this specifically through songs that have a very heavy focus on Scripture. I love worship music. I especially love hymns and songs that use passages of Scripture as either the motivation or the entirety of their text. What I want to challenge you to do today, and maybe for the next few days, is to focus on the kinds of songs that are based in God's Word. After all, the purpose of this book is rediscovering our passion and joy for God and the Bible. While praise music in all forms is profitable, even music that grows out of biblical concepts while maybe not directly referencing it, I want your heart tuned to God and His Word for this exercise.

How do you do this? Searching for these types of songs can be tricky, especially if it's new to you. I've tried to make this as simple as I can, but admittedly you may have to do a little hunting.

You may be asking, "How do I find music based on Scripture?" Great question.

To make this as easy as possible, I've created a Spotify playlist of songs that use Scripture as their basis. All you need to do is open the Spotify app and navigate to the "search" function. In the search field, type in "Wake Up: Songs From Scripture."

You should see the playlist come up. Click on the playlist, and you're good to go. You can even choose to follow it if you want, but you don't have to in order to listen.

Another way to find music that is based on the biblical text is to search for "psalm" in your music app of choice, whether that's Spotify, iTunes, Pandora, Amazon Music, etc. This should pull up a list of songs that uses various psalms as their inspiration.

Our family also has listened to a lot of "Seeds Family Worship" over the years. These songs take Bible verses and passages of Scripture and put them to music. While they are created with children and families in mind, the tunes are ridiculously catchy. You will find yourself quoting Scripture to a fun pop melody before you even realize it.

Once you've found music that is based in Scripture, here's your challenge for today:

FIRST, find a way to listen in a place where you can be intentional in listening to the song's lyrics. I hope engaging with God and His Word through music is a regular part of your life as a Christ-follower. But for this devotional experience, I want to challenge you to really set aside space to listen intently to Scripture through song.

THEN, focus on your response. Music leads us to respond to God in ways that are different than hearing a sermon or reading the Bible. We absorb music differently and, therefore, we respond to it differently. Think about how you are led to respond to God. What phrases or concepts connect with you? What feelings or experiences do these words awaken in you? What is God showing you about Himself through these songs? Be aware of your response. Listen to what your heart and mind are saying back to God.

NEXT, set aside room to respond to God in prayerful conversation. Talk to God. Listen to Him. Allow yourself to be moved by what you're experiencing.

FINALLY, don't forget the importance of reflecting on the truths of what God is trying to teach you about Himself and you. Continue to listen to music over the next few days as an intentional, focused way of encountering God.

PRAYING THE PRAYERS OF
THE BIBLE

No matter how much I understand it from a theological perspective, prayer will always be a wonderful mystery to me. I hope I never lose the wonder of being able to communicate with the holy Creator, the God of the Universe.

Isn't it just wild to think about? We speak words to God, and He hears them. And not only does He hear them, but He also intercedes on our behalf as a result (in accordance with His sovereign plan and will, of course). There really is nothing quite like it. Prayer is a powerful, wonderful, sometimes hard-to-grasp aspect of our relationship with God.

Prayer is awesome. And yet sometimes, if we're honest, we can feel a little lost doing it.

I've had countless moving interactions with God through prayer. I've experienced God answering my prayers more times than I can count. I have connected with God powerfully through prayer. And there are also seasons in my life when it feels like my prayers don't make it out of my head or mouth, much less to the throne room of God. I have over the years of my relationship with God been inconsistent in my prayer. I have been frustrated by prayer. I have been disappointed by prayer, and I have been left wondering if my prayers were heard, much less answered. If you've ever felt this or anything similar to this, you're not alone.

Prayer can sometimes be a struggle. And that's why I am so thankful for the record of real prayers spoken by real people in the Bible. These prayers work like a model for us, giving fresh expression to our desires, especially in moments when we're struggling with what or how to pray.

Early on in this book, you had the chance to practice praying using Scripture as your guide. As we wrap up this book, I want to offer you the same chance, but with a slightly different angle. I want you not to try and insert yourself in the general requests we see in many of the psalms, but instead, to place yourself in the prayers of people reaching out to God in prayer, rooted in the very specific context of their lives.

It is easy for us to forget that the characters we encounter in Scripture were real people with real problems. Their lives were deep and rich and complex, just like ours. They had trials as we do. They experienced frustration. They fell short of God's desire for them. They experienced God's goodness and grace. And in all of these experiences, they responded to God in prayer.

Today I want you to be able to draw upon the rich experiences of some of the characters of the Bible and make their prayer your prayer. I believe this is an important way of approaching God and His Word, especially as we are people seeking to draw closer to God. When we align our desires with the desires of those we encounter in Scripture, it gives us a great hope that God will meet us in the manner in which He met those in the books of the Bible. God is faithful. He always answers our prayers according to His sovereignty and perfect plan. We can go to God in prayer, knowing that we are heard and that our concerns are important to God. Modeling prayer after those who have gone before us gives us confidence that God hears us as He heard them.

HERE'S YOUR CHALLENGE FOR TODAY:

FIRST, look at the list below of some of the most well-known prayers of the Bible. Look for yourself in the descriptions. Are you dealing with something one of the characters below dealt with? Read through the list and allow yourself to choose a prayer that speaks to where you are right now.

- Hannah praising God for answering her prayer in 1 Samuel 2:1-10

- David's prayer for deliverance from a period of trial and distress in Psalm 3

- David's prayer of repentance in Psalm 51:1-17

- David's prayer of surrender to God in Psalm 139

- Jonah's prayer for God to rescue him from his place of experiencing God's judgment in Jonah 2:1-9

- Jesus teaching the disciples the Lord's Prayer in Matthew 6:9-13

- Mary's prayer thanking God for His blessing in Luke 1:46-49

- The tax collector's simple prayer for forgiveness in Luke 18:13

- The apostle's prayer for boldness in Acts 4:29-30

- Paul's prayer for spiritual strength in Ephesians 3:14-20

- Paul's prayer for spiritual wisdom for the Ephesians in Ephesians 1:15-20

- Paul's prayer that God would continue His work in the lives of the Philippians in Philippians 1:2-7

- Paul's prayer for a righteous love in Philippians 1:9-11

- Paul's prayer for wisdom in Colossians 1:9-12

THEN, find the prayer in the Bible. Read the passage surrounding the prayer to get your bearings and to capture a little bit of the context.

NEXT, go to God in prayer, praising Him for who He is. Worship Him. Honor Him. Then, transition into the prayer you see in Scripture. Pray the words as if they are yours, knowing that you're praying words that God gave us as an example of how to reach out to Him. Hear your own needs and desires in what you pray. Be confident that you are connecting with God in an ancient and timeless way and that He hears you.

FINALLY, spend time in silent reflection listening to what God impresses upon you. Thank God that He hears our prayers and honors our desire to draw closer to Him. Consider referring back to the prayer throughout the day. (Or, pray through another prayer on the list.)

CLOSING

"Bibles laid open, millions of surprises." So said seventeenth-century poet and priest George Herbert. My prayer is that you have finished this book and that because of your interaction with the Bible, you can echo Herbert's wonder in what the Bible reveals about God and you.

God is so far above us, so unlike us, so majestic. And while the Bible is to be praised and revered, the very nature of it is that it is approachable. The Bible is God's plan to make Himself known to us as much as He will. It is a remarkable act on His part that He would lovingly provide a way for us to truly learn all that He would have us learn about Him this side of eternity. It is an amazing treasure.

I pray that as you stand having worked through this book, your faith has been impacted. I pray that you have encountered God in ways that maybe you haven't before. I pray that as a result, you feel nearer to God and that your joy for Him is renewed and increased. Ultimately, I find myself praying that many years from now, you can look back at this experience and see it as a significant spiritual marker in your life as a Christ-follower.

Those are big prayers, aren't they? And yet, I can boldly make them without arrogance or ego, knowing that if any of them come true, I had very little to do with it! My desire for this book all along was that it helped present God and His Word to you in a way that awakened you to the richness and fullness of the Scriptures. If you have been moved, if this experience has been beneficial, it is only because you have come close to God and been changed as a result. That's how God works.

My challenge to you is that you would build off your newfound closeness with God and that you would see this time as a catalyst for a season in your life when you are pursuing God with great passion and commitment. Keep growing. Keep leaning into who God is and what He is doing in your life. Continue to listen to what God is revealing about Himself in and through His Word.

More than anything, don't lose sight of the "joy of your salvation." God is near to you. He is always near. And as you have learned through this journey, you have nothing to do but to draw near to Him to confirm this truth.

ABOUT THE AUTHOR

ANDY BLANKS

Andy Blanks is the Publisher and Co-Founder of YM360 and Iron Hill Press. A former Marine, he has worked in youth ministry, mostly in the field of publishing, for nearly 15 years. During that time, Andy has led the development of some of the most popular Bible study curriculum and discipleship resources in the country. He has authored numerous books, Bible studies, and articles, and regularly speaks at events and conferences, both for adults and teenagers. But Andy's passion is communicating the transforming truth of the God's Word, which he does in his local church on a weekly basis.

Andy and his wife, Brendt, were married in 2000. They have four children, three girls and one boy.

A 3-PART DEVOTIONAL EXPERIENCE
DESIGNED TO HELP YOU BECOME A DISCIPLE OF CHRIST.
IN A WORD, TO KNOW GOD AND MAKE HIM KNOWN.

The *New/Next/Now* Discipleship Bundle provides three powerful devotional experiences to help you grow from a new believer to an authentic disciple of Christ.

NEW: FIRST STEPS FOR NEW CHRIST-FOLLOWERS

One of the most used new believer resources in youth ministry, this powerful 4-week devotional experience will help new believers get off to a strong start on their new journey with Christ.

NEXT: GROWING A FAITH THAT LASTS

4-week devotional will help you take ownership of your faith. NEXT will teach: Why it's important to own your faith, What life's purpose has to do with God's mission, How to build spiritual habits that last a lifetime, and How to use the influence you already have for Christ.

NOW: IMPACTING YOUR WORLD FOR CHRIST (RIGHT NOW!)

You have the amazing potential to impact your world for Christ, not just some time in the future ... but right NOW! Today. Your world is rich with opportunities to share the hopeful message of the Gospel, and to show people the amazing difference Christ can make in their lives. Now will help you make the most of these opportunities!

TO VIEW SAMPLES OF *NEW, NEXT & NOW* AND TO ORDER, GO TO YM360.COM/DEVOBUNDLE

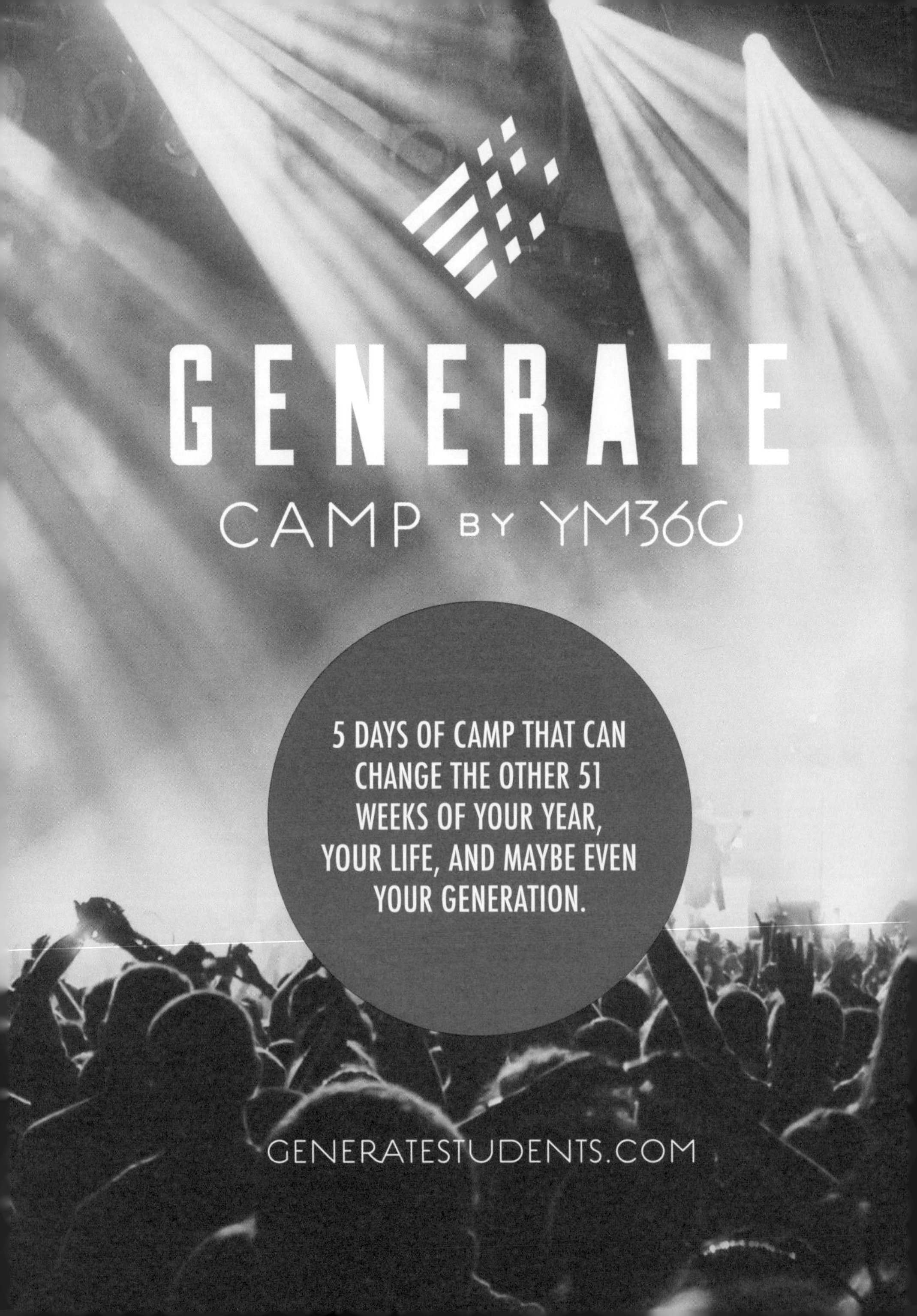
GENERATE
CAMP BY YM360
5 DAYS OF CAMP THAT CAN CHANGE THE OTHER 51 WEEKS OF YOUR YEAR, YOUR LIFE, AND MAYBE EVEN YOUR GENERATION.
GENERATESTUDENTS.COM